To Evelyn With

Dennis + Ginger

Tips

&

TALES

*An Indiana Journalist
Reflects on Craft and Career*

Dennis Royalty

Granite Publishing
Prescott & Dover
2021

"There is no greater agony than bearing an untold story inside you."—Maya Angelou

Copyright

Imprint: Granite Publishing January 2021
Line Ed.: Pat Fogarty

ISBN: 978-1-950105-30-4

Granite Publishing
Prescott & Dover

98765432
First Edition

Printed in the United States of America
Cover Design—Pat Fogarty

HBBXNY 1551065906

"It was while making newspaper deliveries, trying to miss the bushes and hit the porch, that I first learned the importance of accuracy in journalism."—Charles Osgood

Dedication

To Ginger, Kelsey, Andrew & Sheri

Reviews

"*Tips and Tales*" is a must-read if you want to be a better writer—or if you just love great journalism. Dennis Royalty offers thoughtful, humorous insights into the stories he reported, wrote, and edited over his stellar career, along with his best writing tips. I always knew Dennis was the finest of journalists and mentors, and his book proves it."

. . . . Linda Graham Caleca—award winning veteran journalist and writing coach

"It's not mere blandishment to invoke the great craft gurus such as William Zinsser and E.B. White in describing Dennis Royalty's "*Tips and Tales.*" The longtime newspaper professional and dedicated solo journalist interweaves astute advice with deftly rendered accounts of career and life moments that are as moving and entertaining as they are instructive. Both the neophyte and the veteran of non-fiction writing can profit from Royalty's breakdown of the X's and O's of the game, and one hardly needs to be in the journalistic arena to enjoy his reminiscences of adolescence in small-town Indiana, friendship with baseball legend Carl Erskine, a complicated relationship with that sportswriters' scourge, Bob Knight, and so much more. Good advice, good reading. "*Tips and Tales*" is a welcome addition to my freelancer's toolbox."

. . . Dan Carpenter—prolific freelance writer, former newspaper columnist and author of four books:

Introduction

I had a slow news day at *The Indianapolis Star's* Purdue-Lafayette Bureau back in the 1970s. The mail brought a new Purdue University telephone directory, so I leafed through it, seeking inspiration.

At the end of the phone book there was something peculiar.

Following the usual A to Z listings came a mystifying category I'd not seen before. Centered on Page 179 was the number 2, with a single name and number posted beneath it:

2angelo, Mario Michael.

Bingo. I had a story. My reporting instincts turned Michael 2angelo into a brief news article, headlined "Student at Purdue is Only a Number."

As you've likely guessed, this was a mistake attributed to a nameless computer. Student Michael M. Angelo had become Michael 2angelo!

As for my own somewhat unusual last name, I was born into Royalty on September 23, 1949, to Dennis Marion Royalty and Kathleen Barnhart Royalty.

My formative years weren't all that formative in science, math, and foreign languages. But I did show an ability to express myself in writing, speech, and journalism classes. I was encouraged and appreciated by wonderful teachers at Frankfort (Indiana) High School and Indiana University. So I went on to make a living putting words together, as I'm doing here.

This book is about life experiences, from high school and IU to the former Bloomington (Indiana) *Courier-Tribune*, and then on to my longest career stint. That was

27 years at *The Indianapolis Star*, the state's largest circulation newspaper, beginning with six years at the Purdue-Lafayette Bureau and including a decade as city editor.

Along the way, I've worked with many talented writers, editors, and writing coaches. Wisdom from them and from talented communicators at Eli Lilly and Company (where I spent 14 years before retiring) is too good not to share here in the form of writing advice that follows each chapter.

In the pages ahead I hope you'll find reasons to smile, to commiserate, to reflect on your own life. And to gain from what I've learned about reporting, writing, and editing.

Before you begin, an admission: I've used direct quotes in some places that are based on memories, letters, and notes kept over the years. I've done my best to ensure that the quotes accurately reflect the intent of what was said. And I've checked myself with various sources noted in the book's Afterword.

You're about to read life experiences, tips from a life in journalism, and some of the columns I had a lot of fun putting together for *The Star*. I hope you enjoy what follows and, along the way, gather useful nuggets for your own writing.

You 2, Mario M. Angelo.

Contents

Breaking In

"Progress is crisis-oriented," a wise man once told me. It's a great saying, so often true.

I only wish I'd heard it prior to 1966, when it might have offered some consolation to a fuzzy-faced teen working at Schnaible's Drug Store in Frankfort, Indiana.

Schnaible's was my first job, unless you count delivering *The Denver Post* when we lived in Colorado.

I'll get to the crisis part in a minute. First, the setup. This story begins when my parents urged me to earn money for college during my junior year in high school.

Saving at 75 cents an hour was realistic in '66, given I lived at home, there wasn't a whole lot to spend money on, and even if you did, baseball cards were a nickel a pack. My pal, Andy Mitchell, already was a stock boy at Schnaible's—so there was added incentive to work there.

"Stock boy" actually was "do-anything-boy" on nights and weekends. We added price tags to everything, from aspirin to shoe polish, and carefully positioned new stock behind the old as we shelved items in neat little rows. But the job also required everything from bagging for the cashier to working the register when Marguerite took a break, to cleaning the stockroom and the bathrooms, and—very important to owner/pharmacist Fred Schnaible—helping customers with a smile.

Smile I did, but I also tilted toward harmless smart-alecky at times. This behavior was limited, usually, to shoppers I knew as they entered Schnaible's with a "help me find it" expression.

"Looking for Alka-Seltzer?" I'd say. *"See that Coke machine back in the corner? It's nowhere near there."*

(Fear not: I quickly steered folks to their quest. No harm done, and a little boredom lifted for me.)

Excitement came to Schnaible's every six weeks or so with the arrival of the Kiefer-Stewart truck, bringing sales merchandise ahead of our ad in the *Frankfort Morning Times.*

That's when Andy and I had to hustle. We needed to unpack what the truck brought to the stockroom, then get it marked and displayed before the ad hit *The Times.*

I'll never forget Bon Ami cleanser, priced at 9 cents a can. Kiefer-Stewart unloaded what seemed like hundreds of the round containers, each invariably coated in the flour-like cleanser. We got them priced and shelved on time, but wore Bon-Ami powder for the rest of the shift.

Andy and I stacked Kiefer-Stewart boxes floor-to-ceiling in the stockroom. One day, we giddily yanked open a large container marked "Super Balls" that had been precariously stacked atop other boxes, within reach but at least 8 feet up.

A cascade of bouncy orbs ensued in all directions. Dozens hopped about as if they were alive, making such a commotion that Mr. Schnaible abandoned his post to check out the noise.

This was one of the rare times when Fred Schnaible looked over his bifocals at us, red-faced and exasperated. The rubbery balls not only caromed off his legs, but, worse, some bounced beyond and into the store.

Who knew Super Balls didn't come in individual packaging?

The Super Ball episode aside, Mr. Schnaible was tolerant, forgiving, and kind. He and another good-natured pharmacist, Dave Decker, not only managed the pharmacy but ran the entire store, dividing a seven-day workweek. In their eyes, I was a conscientious worker, arriving on time, a self-starter. Schnaible's seemed a perfect fit for me.

Until, that is, pharmacist Steve Decker arrived— Dave's younger brother.

Mr. Schnaible had another store in Lafayette to look after, so needed more help. Steve was tall (maybe 6-3) and thin, with a drill sergeant-looking crew cut and personality to match. The fact that the pharmacy area was built a couple of stairs higher than the rest of the store made him seem all the more intimidating.

The honeymoon was over for Andy and me. Me, especially.

"DEN-NIS." "Oh, DEN-NIS!" Steve's voice carried to the supermarket next door and the parking lot beyond.

A task hadn't been done to his satisfaction. I was in the crosshairs as I hurried to his pharmacy perch.

"How long had I been working here? What else did I need to have explained to me?" On and on he went. Before Steve, coming to work was pleasant. His demanding style changed that. And it kept me on edge.

I can't blame what happened next on Steve Decker. But in my defense, I was doing a lot of looking over my shoulder when he ran the store, my confidence wavering.

And so it was when I confronted the dreaded routine of refilling distilled water bottles.

Frankfort was well known for its hard water, so distilled water sales were high. Schnaible's carried 1-gallon glass bottles that were returned after use. It fell to Andy and me to peel off the old labels, affix new ones, and refill the bottles.

Refilling them meant pouring water into each bottle from sizable 5-gallon glass jugs.

At this point, I must confess that arm strength has never been, well, a strength for me. When a 5-gallon glass jug was full, it was all I could do to hoist it in the air, aim it at a glass funnel placed in the mouth of an empty bottle on the floor, and pour in a gallon's worth.

Once the empty was full, I'd remove the funnel, cap the newly-filled bottle, and repeat the same hefting chore until enough 1-gallon distilled water bottles were ready to restock the shelves.

Along came a Saturday morning where things weren't going well. Andy was off and I had much to do. Leaving the distilled water refilling to his next shift wasn't an option. Naturally, when it came time to refill empties, the 5-gallon jug was completely full. This maximized the degree-of-difficulty for me.

I placed the glass funnel into the mouth of an empty and lifted the large jug, staggering under its weight. Distilled water surged forth, slopping beyond the funnel. Suddenly I was off-balance, grappling with a-now-slippery 5-gallon jug.

Out of control and out of my hands it went, like a dirigible crashing to earth. Only in this case, the massive jug slammed into the glass funnel and glass bottle below, smashing them to pieces.

A resounding crash brought pounding footsteps from the pharmacy section, just outside the stockroom.

Steve Decker's eyes caught me at my worst, fumbling to retrieve hunks of glass but skidding on a flooded floor.

"IDIOT!" "IMBECILE!"

"Clean up this mess right away! Get the rest of those bottles filled!"

But then Steve realized there could be no more distilled bottles filled this day, or any day in the near future. That's because our glass funnel was in shards on the floor. Schnaible's had no other suitable funnel for the task.

"Now you've done it," he thundered. Only an influx of customers at the pharmacy counter halted the onslaught, and prevented Steve Decker from seeing tears in my eyes.

It didn't take Mom and Dad long to realize something was up when I got home. After some blubbering and consoling, Dad produced hope.

"I think we've got similar funnels at work....let me check."

Back he came from the National Seal plant with not one but two funnels....a glass one, similar to what I'd broken, and a same-size plastic funnel. A godsend!

I couldn't wait to get back to the store. Steve was alone in the pharmacy area when I rushed up to him.

"Look what I've got," I said meekly, pointing to a paper bag I carried.

"What now?" he barked, descending the stairs.

Triumphantly, I reached into the bag. I would show him!

Inside, I had sleeved the funnels. I grabbed one and whisked them out, triumphantly.

"Here you go," I beamed.

But I was gripping only the top edge of the plastic funnel.

From beneath it slipped the glass funnel.

Which plunged to the tile floor, end over end.

And smashed into pieces!

Teeny, tiny pieces. Glass everywhere.

I froze.

Steve did too, eyes bulging.

Finally, I managed a gasp, incredulous. And awaited Mount Vesuvius to explode.

He did. But in laughter.

Loud, belly-grabbing, raucous laughter. Recognition of the absurdity-of-it-all kind of laughter.

And then he touched my shoulder—not to send me reeling, but in a caring way.

Steve Decker wasn't laughing at me, he said.

Stuff happens. Everything will be OK.

"But how about getting a broom and a dustpan, to clean this up?"

Things were never the same between me and Steve Decker after that. Instead, they got better, much better.

We still had a plastic funnel. He even thanked me for bringing it in.

So, from the apparent worst, progress. Crisis-oriented progress, to be sure.

But a good kind of progress, as progress so often is.

Writing Tip #1—Keep a Daily Journal

It seems odd that my first recommendation for writers in this book is of the "do as I say, not as I do" variety.

But here goes.

Keep a daily journal or diary. Not only will this mean flexing your writing muscles at least once a day, a good thing, but it will also provide material, and inspiration, for your own book.

The more specific your journal entries, the better. Describe what you lived through each day, what you felt, and why the journal entries are meaningful. Be as precise as possible. You'll be grateful for that later.

I haven't kept my own journal. I've regretted not doing so, particularly when I decided to write this memoir.

What has worked for me is a packrat-like habit of saving my newspaper clippings and other writings.

In addition to scrapbooks filled with clips, I've kept files bulging with old school papers, writing tips, correspondence, and copies of a Christmas letter I've written for decades. These have proven a gold mine in writing this book, although they're not nearly as comprehensive as recording your daily life.

So keep your own journal, no matter how much a drudgery it seems. I wish I had.

Highway Robbery

The professor marched to the front of the room, papers stuffed under an arm.

Creative writing students perked from slouch to straighten. This was a big day in Rocky Blodgett's English 131 class.

"Rocky" was my nickname for Prof. Blodgett. I can't recall why, or his real first name. But I do remember this day more than most in my time at Indiana University.

Thirty-some of us were about to learn grades for our first assignment of the semester. We'd submitted compositions the previous week, striving for clever, profound, fresh, or whatever else would register favorably on Rocky's big-stakes homework.

The stakes were big because there would be just two lengthy papers to produce over the semester. Each would be worth 25 percent of our letter grade. The remaining 50 percent would hinge on a paper assigned and written during the two-hour final exam.

I'd seated myself in the front row as we awaited the return of our first papers. Watching Blodgett weave through desks, delivering graded compositions, it was easy to read student faces as they learned their marks.

I was confident of a respectable grade. (Hey, I majored in journalism.) But my curiosity turned to concern when Rocky strode past my desk.

He'd handed back everyone's paper but mine.

I rose to ask why. But I was too late. Now he was poised to address the class.

"I'll start today by reading the most outstanding essay," he said. Then he fingered the bridge of his glasses, took a deep breath, and began.

The first words seemed familiar. Then, it became clear:

These were **my** words.

Classmates didn't recognize the mystery author, of course. Still, I felt embarrassed while Rocky read on, especially at the end when he left his seat and ceremoniously dropped the paper on my desk with an encouraging, "Well done!"

Rousing applause followed, echoing throughout the building.

Not really. Still, this was a big-time ego-enhancer, so welcome in my early college days of highs and lows (for the latter, see: Economics 201 and Psychology 101).

Back to Blodgett's classroom. Now it's a month later, following the second 25 percent writing chore. And here came *déjà vu*. I thought.

Assignment 2 had been in his hands for a week. Once again Rocky strode briskly to the front of the room, 30 or so papers arm-crooked for the trip.

Pausing briefly to straighten the pile, he again weaved through our desks. Looks of anticipation covered faces.

Once again, I'm seated in the front row. And, once more, Blodgett didn't return my paper as he headed to the front of the room to pronounce, once again, that a single paper stood out. We must all hear another example of exceptional writing, he said.

Expectant eyes swiveled in my direction.

Aw, shucks. Here we go again.

But...but....but....as Blodget read on, these **weren't my words**.

This time Blodgett crowned a female classmate as the next acclaimed writing champion.

That's OK, I guess. But where was my paper? I had to wait through a 45-minute lecture to find out. When class was dismissed, I confronted Rocky.

"I returned all the papers I had," he said. "You sure you turned yours in?"

("Oh, yeah, Blodgett, I decided to skip this paper after I aced the first one. It's just too humbling when you keep reading my stuff aloud.")

Thankfully, Rocky couldn't hear that thought bubble.

"No, I turned it in," I sputtered. "I wrote this one even better than the first."

Rocky said he'd search his office desk and check at home, too, in case he'd misplaced my work.

No luck. He'd lost the paper, though he never admitted it.

"I will accept your word that you turned in the second assignment," he said. "We'll judge you for the semester with your first paper and the final."

This plan concerned me, even though I was riding the A train. A misstep on the exam would send my grade the only direction it could—lower.

But the decision was locked. My accomplishments would ride on just two grades.

There isn't a happy ending. Rocky Blodgett judged my final exam as B-worthy, making the course grade a B-plus. This was the outcome despite the fact I had a creative writing paper judged so good that it was read to the entire class.

Unfortunately for me, at that time the university counted a **B**-plus as a grade of **B** on my transcript. B-level grades earned the equivalent of 3 points out of 4 on a 4-point scale.

Highway robbery!

Never mind the blanket **A** that I was awarded in another writing course by a very charitable professor, or some "minus" grades that were rounded up in my favor over my college career.

You did me wrong, Rocky.

Writing Tip #2—Read, Read, Read

Good writers are insatiable readers or should be. Reading every day exposes you to different styles and techniques and enhances learning.

So gobble up books, magazines, newspapers, and news websites. Jot notes to yourself of techniques you admire (creating a separate section in your journal or diary would be good for this).

Reading helps you identify authors and publications you respect, but don't stop there. Widen your experiences by reading other points of view.

Before writing this book, I asked a speaker at a professional writers' meeting what would best help me prepare for the task.

Her answer: read memoirs by other people, especially those written by communicators. (This sent me scurrying to the library. I picked up *"Reporter,"* by Pulitzer Prize-winning author Seymour "Sy" Hersh, and I recommend his book as a good read and a helpful learning tool).

Thanks for the inspiration for my own book, Sy.

The Last All-Nighter

They call it cramming, pulling an all-nighter, "waiting till the last minute," or, more simply, procrastination.

Ranking the silly things I did in college, all-night studying for a final exam neared the top.

Doesn't work. Didn't work. Not for me.

Tom Benton and I knew we were in trouble as our final neared for the "History of Western Civilization" at Indiana University. So we staked out a dorm lounge, bought snacks, and settled in for desperation mode.

"Benjie" was a flop-haired guy who looked like a high school junior. Fifty years later, he's probably still yanking out his driver's license to earn senior discounts.

Studying came easily to him. So why were we a pair that night?

In 1968 I was a sophomore, he a freshman. Like me, Benjie had overestimated how prepared he was in "Western Civ." Studying for other finals had shoved this one to the back burner for both of us.

It's foolish to hope you can cram everything you need to know into six or seven hours. But we were headstrong dudes. Never mind the course text was huge, telephone-bookish. We were convinced that by 7:30 a.m., we'd be ready.

And so we crammed.

A lot of serious work happened in the first hour or two, from maybe 10 to midnight. We quizzed each other, reviewed earlier tests and assignments, and strained to remember what the prof had emphasized. Determination reigned.

Staying up late wasn't all that unusual for college types, so we figured this would be a walk in the park.

The clock passed 1, then 2 a.m. before fatigue began to take hold.

A bathroom trip found the hallways quiet. Doors were closed and slumber ruled for sensible students. Envy brought temptation: let's give it another hour or two, catch a nap, and head to the final.

But we kept on. That's because our studying made it painfully apparent that what we didn't know reached swimming pool depths.

So, can't stop now. Can't stop until it's time to head to Ballantine Hall.

Concentration became the enemy, or lack of it. First the atmosphere turned giddy, humorous. Then it shifted to testy, argumentative. The need for sleep had drained any spirit of goodwill.

With class notes spilled across tables, chairs, and ottomans. I'd strayed across the room, leaving my book behind. I asked Benjie to hand it over.

"Get your own," he snapped. Then, on second thought, he grabbed the text and flung it my way, with force.

Pages tore through the air. Dozens separated from the softback cover, unable to survive the cartwheeling journey in my direction.

I was furious.

Expletive, expletive! I leaped up and grabbed what was left of the book, bounding toward Benjie. He'd pay for his insolence.

Then, in mid-charge, a revelation.

I noticed a name scrawled on the torn cover.

"Tom Benton," it said.

He'd thrown *his own* book at me.

My gleeful howl seemed to make the evening worth it. Not so. My triumph wore off quickly with the realization that we still weren't ready, and exhausted to boot.

We dragged ourselves to the final, a 2-hour ordeal. All those facts about western civilization competed with keeping my eyes open. As I yawned repeatedly, a teaching assistant approached. Did I need some coffee?

The upshot: My performance cost me an entire letter grade.

I learned a lesson that had nothing to do with academics. It was a lesson in preparation, or lack of sensibly preparing. My habits had to change, and they did.

A wise colleague later described the importance of planning and personal discipline like this: "Give yourself the opportunity to fail—and recover." Great advice.

So, this was my first and last all-nighter.

Benjie? I bet he aced it. He was one of those fall-in-the-hay-find-pony types.

I would end this tale right here, but doing so without passing along another cramming episode would rob you of a story that makes me smile.

College buddy John Messina, still a close friend, relates:

"It was my astrophysics final, A401 or A402. This was my major, so I wanted to make sure I was ready and really knew the material.

"I had my own room, so staying up all night wasn't a problem. The final was at 7:30 a.m. the next morning. I kept studying until about 5:30 when I was satisfied that I was ready.

"I decided to take a nap so I could be fresh. I'd get up at 7 and have plenty of time to walk to the test.

"**But I woke up around 8:30!** I was in a state of shock. Oh no! I may have missed the final exam in my major!

"I don't remember if I'd forgotten to set the alarm, or if I just slept through it. But I dashed over to the classroom, now around 9 a.m. for a test that was supposed to end at 9:30.

"I barged in and told the prof 'I'm so sorry. I overslept. Is there anything I can do?'

"I was feeling really lousy, especially when the prof, Dr. Honeycutt, said he'd take me to another room to work on it. I figured he'd make me do the entire test in 30 minutes.

"But he didn't.

"Honeycutt opened the door, and there were six other students sitting there. Turns out we were all there for the same reason."

John and the rest got to take the test in full. Unlike me, he knew his stuff, from general relativity to problems involving gravitational orbiting to identifying different types of telescopes. His "A" locked in the same grade for the semester.

At least *he* had a happy ending.

Writing Tip #3—Twenty Questions

Preparation is essential, whether you intend to write an article, short story, fiction, or non-fiction. Thorough preparation as a reporter or researcher best positions you to be a compelling storyteller.

Pulitzer Prize-winning reporter Bill Anderson shared great advice when I was a rookie at *The Indianapolis Star*. Bill was a tenacious police reporter. He told me that, for every assignment, he would scribble (or mentally prepare) 20 questions for news sources. He did this routinely as he raced to cover a crime scene. That readied him for seizing control of interviews when he arrived.

Intensive preparation is even more important when the subject isn't breaking news. Know all you can about who you'll be interviewing. Carefully familiarize yourself with all topics to be explored. Your mission is to add depth and meaning to what readers already know.

Sandy Nelson of Arizona writes mystery fiction (as S. Resler Nelson). Before writing, she queries police and other experts about how they investigate, how they protect crime scenes, how they conduct target interviews, and so on. The results are evident in her Luke Hudson series—believability and credibility. So yes, careful preparation applies even to writing fiction.

Accuracy and authenticity win readers over to your side. Preparation takes time, but it pays off.

What Are You Doing This Summer?

This is a story I've told dozens of times over the last 45 years. I'm happy to share it with a new audience.

Pay particular attention if you're young and looking to improve your career prospects. The example that follows could benefit your journey, as it did mine.

Life was busy but happy in early 1970, my junior year at Indiana University. I'd gotten better at balancing classwork while writing and editing for *The Indiana Daily Student*. I tried unsuccessfully to convince a publication board that I should become the next editor-in-chief. But that setback wasn't awful, given that I was a finalist at a respected journalism school.

On this particular day, I was cruising through the noisy newsroom at Ernie Pyle Hall, where typewriters banged out the day's news.

That's when Marge Blewett stopped me.

Part instructor, part placement bureau, part den mother, Marge Blewett was as familiar in Pyle Hall as the wire service machines.

"What are you doing this summer?" she asked.

"Going back to Frankfort," I said, "living with my folks and doing factory work so I can afford my senior year."

Not the right answer, Marge's glare showed.

Returning to factory work? "No, you're not."

***

Marge Blewett took pride in placing journalism students at newspapers around the country. She knew the best way to land a job in the field was to gain experience through an internship.

It should have been obvious to me to line up my own. But I was oblivious.

I had taken for granted that I would be back at the National Seal factory, using my trusty micrometer to test automotive parts. I would once again be a quality control technician thanks to my personnel manager father. It was decent money and paid college expenses that my folks didn't cover.

Quality control had been a white-collar job between my sophomore and junior years. It represented a step up from the first factory post Dad arranged for me after my freshman year. That was assembly-line work at Frankfort's P.R. Mallory plant, a grimy chore of washing metal shavings off tuners in the television parts process. That highly regimented work was interrupted only when buzzers signaled 10-minute breaks, 20-minute lunch, or go-home time.

At Mallory, I once accidentally overloaded a bucketful of heavy nail-like tuners. My job was to wash them using a centrifugal-force machine that, when switched on, drained away metal shavings while drying the tuners.

My overload sent the lopsided bucket spinning out of control at a high speed. Tuners that ordinarily were pinned against the sides of the rapidly spinning bucket sailed out of the top like missiles. Bang, **bang!**

Steely projectiles shot across my workspace and into others, slamming against equipment, walls, everywhere. It was a storm of flying nails.

I dived for cover beneath the top-of-bucket level. Then I crawled, froggy-style, to the on-off switch.

I was grateful the foreman didn't see this happen, or OSHA. Luckily, I'd started this particular load as everyone was heading to break. My "break" was spent scooping up wayward tuners.

Washing them was steamy, arduous work. It was much more physically demanding than quality control at National Seal, though both were monotonous routines that left me clock-watching.

Reading this you must wonder "Why, oh why" didn't I have an internship in mind for the journalism field I cherished? Decades later, it's inexplicable. Chalk it up to scatterbrained youth.

Which makes me so grateful for what followed.

***

"Good news," Marge said. "I talked to Larry Connor. You're going to be a summer intern at *The Indianapolis Star*."

She asked me to phone City Editor Connor to work out the details. I learned that I would be a general assignment reporter on the 1:30 p.m. to 10:30 p.m. shift, commuting the hour or so to Indy from Frankfort.

Just like that, I was bound for the largest newspaper in the state. I would cover the news and learn from veteran reporters and editors. The salary would cover my share of college bills.

Marge Blewett had changed my life.

***

My first day interning at *The Star* was made easier because three new full-time reporters started work the same day. One, Monte Trammer, later became a deputy managing editor at *USA Today* and an executive in Florida, also serving on the board of directors of the National Association of Black Journalists. Another was Bonnie Britton, an excellent feature writer who for years was *The Star's* movie critic. I've lost track of the other guy, a reporter named Jack Booth.

I list them because I had the good fortune of sharing rookie status instead of bearing it all myself. Throughout the summer I answered phones and wrote dozens of obituaries, which then were reported by *The Star* without making families pay to publish them—a practice that, regrettably, has changed.

Softball assignments for me and the other newcomers quickly turned to more responsibility when we filled in for vacationing staffers. By summer's end, I was producing respectable bylined stories. I felt like a valued reporter at a major metropolitan newspaper.

Monte, Bonnie, Jack, and I bloomed on a staff that ranged from impressive role models to a few scribes of the "hanger-on" variety. That was noticeable for one old-timer who was still at *The Star* thanks to a reputation earned over decades. One evening I was searching for supplies when I discovered a bottle of whiskey in a shared drawer next to him.

Much of my copy was edited by Helen Connor (no relation to Larry). Helen was a stickler for accuracy blessed with the personality of a kind teacher. She was a pro's pro, unfazed by deadline chaos and a splendid, colorful writer.

It took more than a month to deserve my first byline. Coming from Helen, it felt like a championship ribbon at the fair.

My general assignments were wide-ranging. I wrote about a local woman who endured a hijacked airline flight. I covered a school desegregation protest. And I interviewed a veteran who married in wartime and was struggling to bring his Vietnamese wife and child to the U.S.

I took a call from a stringer who had attended the "switching-on" ceremony for a new traffic light in a suburban community. A small crowd watched as the first car entering the intersection cruised through the bright red signal. (This was my breakthrough Page One story, all four paragraphs of it.)

On temporary assignment to suburban coverage, I took what should have been a forgettable excursion to meet a correspondent in nearby Greenfield. The trip turned memorable when the dashboard of a badly neglected staff car tumbled onto my lap.

I remember dragging home to Frankfort after days of relative quiet followed by bursts of deadline action. I was treated like a full-time colleague by reporters and editors I admired, including Larry and Helen, Tom

Keating (who became a well-respected columnist), and political writers Paul Doherty and Bob Mooney.

It was an experience-gaining three months that made it clear: this was the profession for me.

***

Back in Bloomington for my senior year at IU, I delivered bountiful thanks to Marge as I gushed over the experiences I had at *The Star*.

My new role on *The Daily Student* staff didn't work out well under the new editor-in-chief, so I took a part-time job writing sports on weekends for the *Bloomington Courier-Tribune*.

The *C-T* offered me full-time sports-writing after graduation in May of 1971. The job was fulfilling, often exhilarating, and produced lifelong friends. But it lasted only until December 27, 1973, when staffers were summoned to the front of the newsroom. That's when the publisher delivered bad news: the newspaper was folding, unable to sufficiently woo advertisers in competition with the entrenched Bloomington *Herald-Telephone*. This despite the fact that we had been named a Blue Ribbon newspaper by the Hoosier State Press Association.

Many colleagues were jobless for months before landing new work. We received severance packages, mine for nine weeks-worth of paychecks.

Within days I made my first job inquiry to Larry Connor (nickname: Bo), the city editor who had hired me as an intern. "Denny," he said. "I've got one opening, the Lafayette Bureau. And I've got more than 30 applicants. But I'll let you know."

More than 30 applicants? Ugh.

The calendar had barely turned to January when Bo called back. He offered me the job on the basis of what I'd done during my internship. Bo also made a weekly salary offer.

"Is $217.15 OK?" he asked. I was making $135 at the time.

"That will be great," I said.

Later in January, I was on the job, full-time at *The Star*. Between my new salary and severance, I drew checks from two places for weeks.

***

The moral of this tale is obvious, but I'll say it anyway. Get an internship. Then learn, work hard, show what you can do. Volunteer to take on any experience, and let no task be too little for your best effort. Soak up knowledge that will serve you well later.

The door that Blewett and Connor opened for me led to a 27-year career at *The Star*, 10 as city editor. And that experience led to the last 14 years of my working life as a communicator for Eli Lilly and Company.

An internship teaches you whether your path is indeed the one you want to follow, be it in journalism or elsewhere. Bust your tail when you get the opportunity. You'll gain positive references that should move you up the resume pile with future employers. You will be a proven commodity.

Marge Blewett died in 2019 at age 91, but not before receiving the IU School of Journalism's first Distinguished Alumni Award. She excelled in many ways in addition to guiding many, many students to internships and first jobs.

If this example benefits readers of this book, Marge, you will have done it again.

__Marge Blewett and Larry Connor: They changed my life.__

Writing Tip #4—Get Multiple Sources

You must pursue all sides of a story to present the best available truth.

This tip is an essential practice for would-be journalists. Your credibility is at stake if you don't exhaustively pursue all sides of an argument or controversy.

There's an expression in newsrooms that says it all: "Nothing spoils a good story like getting both sides." This is an overstatement, but you get the idea. The newspaper stories I'm most proud of were the result of taking whatever time necessary to get at the truth.

Fairness is a pillar of responsible journalism.

One of the highest compliments I was ever paid came from a Superior Court judge who had authorized a probe of corruption in Tippecanoe County, Indiana.

"You're just like Lt. Columbo," he said after I had followed up with him for the umpteenth time while researching an article. (The judge was referring to the tenacity of a rumpled television detective who kept coming back with questions for suspects and witnesses.)

I cherish that characterization. You should, too, if you aspire to this line of work.

The Bob Knight I Knew

I was at my desk when the phone rang. It was the early 1970s in the sports department of the *Bloomington Courier-Tribune*, my first full-time job after college.

The caller? Bob Knight, IU basketball coach.

The same Bob Knight known for humiliating or ignoring most sportswriters.

I'd become acquainted while covering the IU basketball beat, but this was a surprise. Knight calling me?

The conversation began something like, "Dennis, I don't know what to do about Bob Owens. What do I need to do to get on the same page with this guy?"

Owens was the *Courier-Tribune's* sports editor. He'd spent many years covering the Hurryin' Hoosiers. Knight's contrasting style was a taste yet to be acquired by some, including the veteran sports editor.

I remember Owens cackling when one headline blared, "Hoosiers Snatch Defeat from Jaws of Victory."

So here was Knight asking Mr. Young Pup Sportswriter how to build a better relationship. Flustered, I managed, "He's sitting about 10 feet away. I'll transfer you."

Knight said OK, so I did. Listening to Owens' side of the conversation, it became clear the ice was melting. Knight and Owens made not just a truce but, over time, a friendship.

***

If you're among the millions who cast Knight aside years ago as a profane bully, you might be surprised to read this. While he always had a handful of media favorites, he earned a reputation for belittling journalists or refusing their presence altogether.

But this wasn't the Bob Knight I knew when I covered his arrival and his first two-plus seasons with the Hoosiers. Oh, he was a disciplinarian, prone to bursts of temper and foul language. But was he a strident, off-putting tyrant? Not then.

I introduced myself in late summer/early fall of 1971. Knight wasn't quite 31 when he arrived in Bloomington. I wasn't yet 22, having graduated from IU in May.

I shared the IU football and basketball beats at the *C-T*. I immediately recognized the tall (6-5), thin new coach from his photos.

Knight was watching a pickup game that included players he would inherit. These players would join him in inaugurating what has become one of the most widely known arenas in college basketball, Assembly Hall.

He smiled at me, and was cordial. Knight said he'd help me however he could.

Our writer/coach relationship would last until late 1973, when it came to a jarring end.

***

Knight kept his promise to help me. But then, in a fit of anger, he fired a basketball at me.

Here's what happened. I was given access to team practices, which was a very big deal in learning how Bob Knight basketball was played.

If you've seen *"Hoosiers"* you'll remember Coach Norman Dale excluding Hickory residents from practice because he tolerated no interference. Dale was created as Knight-like in many respects.

This was one of them. Class was in session when IU practiced. Knight demanded concentration and quiet. If not for sneaker-squeaking, player-panting, and calling out screens, you could have been sitting in a library.

Except for one thing: Knight's teachings, often followed by "Do it again until we get it right."

Rebukes stung as he reached exasperation. There was no mistaking his standards.

It's easiest to remember those outbursts, but they seldom dominated practice. Knight mostly coached in a way reminiscent of my best teachers.

Only a privileged few were allowed to observe from the stands. I painstakingly abided by his demand for silence.

But one day, as I sat 30 or so rows up, I found myself greeted—*out loud, to my horror*—by a new employee from the sports information department. He had somehow made it past the "Closed" signs, unaware of Knight's rule.

Panicked, I shushed. Too late. Coach glanced our way, seething.

For a moment, practice resumed. But more chatting by my oblivious pal led to a volcanic eruption. Roaring disapproval, Knight showed off a pretty amazing arm.

His throw caromed off a seat nearly five rows away. We were then loudly ordered out of the arena.

My friend was miffed. He couldn't understand how a few hushed words could offend. I, on the other hand, was mortified. Not so much by the thrown ball, which probably was more of a warning shot.

I was mortified because what would I tell my boss, Owens, if it turned out I was permanently banned?

So I stuck around in a hallway. I waited until Knight emerged from the dressing room and I explained what happened.

And then I accepted his apology.

Yes, an apology from the same Bob Knight who phoned me at the *C-T* office on a peace-making mission. This was a Knight who could admit fault and realize he'd gone too far.

***

December 1, 1971, was a big day in the history of Indiana basketball. Knight's Hoosiers won their first game in Assembly Hall, 84-77 over Ball State.

December 3, 1971, was a big day in my life. I reported to Fort Knox, Kentucky, for basic training. I had enlisted in the Indiana Army National Guard.

Others covered for me as I missed much of Knight's first season at Indiana. Now I could revert to being a Hoosier fan, as I had been since my teen years at Frankfort, Indiana.

I was in bed after lights out in a Fort Knox barracks when IU traveled to Freedom Hall for a game in nearby Louisville. Playing only its fourth game coached by Knight, IU beat Adolph Rupp's Kentucky Wildcats, 90-89, as Steve Downing scored 47 points and grabbed 25 rebounds—one of the greatest games ever by an Indiana player.

There I was, transistor radio under the covers, rooting like mad for a team I wouldn't get to see in person again for months.

I completed basic training and proceeded to Army clerk school. At last, weekend passes were granted. So I phoned Owens to see if he'd let me cover IU's visit to arch-rival Purdue on Saturday, February 26, 1972. He agreed.

A crowd of 14,123 at Mackey Arena didn't have a lot to cheer about much of the game. IU charged to a 10-point halftime lead and was still in front late, 69-67. But the Hoosiers missed several scoring opportunities and were called for traveling under Purdue's basket with 2 seconds remaining. The final score: 70-69. Tough, tough loss.

Bob Knight nevertheless turned up for postgame remarks to a few of us stationed outside the locker room. Aware that I was away at military training, Knight got a surprise—me. Here I was on weekend pass, using my free time to drive 220 miles and cover IU basketball.

***

Knight was impressed by my covering the Hoosiers at Purdue, but I didn't understand how much until the fall of '72.

That's when the Big Ten held its seventh annual preseason press conference at Chicago. Knight represented IU. I covered for the *C-T*.

By today's standards, the gathering was modest. What has turned into a made-for-TV event with much fanfare was then held in a relatively small ballroom. Coaches took turns providing each team's outlook.

To give an idea of how informal things were, I'd invited my dad. We sat at our own small table roughly 50 feet from the stage.

The Big Ten was really ten those days (now 14 teams). But even just 10 coaches speaking for 10-15 minutes each meant a lot of notebook-scribbling.

I was so busy catching up after the final speaker that I didn't even look up to see Knight standing at our table. It was his first stop before conducting additional one-on-one interviews.

"Den," my dad said. I looked up, surprised, and rose to say hello.

But Knight hadn't come for me. He'd figured out from the stage that this older lookalike was my father. For the next several minutes, I listened awkwardly while he told dad how much he liked my reporting and how he admired the fact that I spent my weekend pass covering IU-Purdue.

***

Talk about not judging a book by its cover: The pint-sized Indiana basketball media guides I've saved from the early 1970s (5- by 7-inch pamphlets) now seem terribly understated given the achievements that followed.

Inside the pages of the 1972-73 and 1973-74 guides were building blocks for greatness. During and after his first season, Knight recruited players who, over the next four seasons, would anchor teams finishing 22-6, 23-5, 31-1, and 32-0. Twice Indiana would reach the Final Four, winning it all in '76 as an undefeated champion. There hasn't been another undefeated NCAA champ since.

As good as those players were, Knight's role as motivator and strategist made it all work.

I'm not breaking news when I say that Knight's drive for perfection had a regrettable side. Even as the team won, his language in public and bench behavior too often ranged from unfortunate to shameful, depending on the beholder.

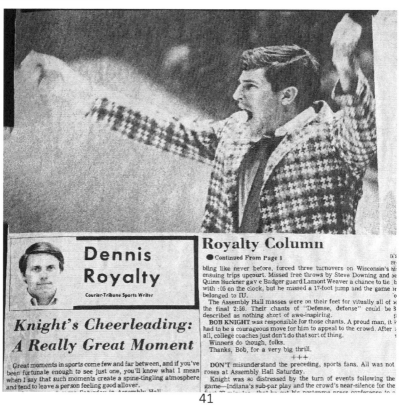

Dennis Royalty

Courier-Tribune Sports Writer

Royalty Column

● Continued From Page 1

bling like never before, forced three turnovers on Wisconsin's ensuing trips upcourt. Missed free throws by Steve Downing and Quinn Buckner gave Badger guard Lamont Weaver a chance to tie with :05 on the clock, but he missed a 17-foot jump and the game belonged to IU.

The Assembly Hall masses were on their feet for virtually all of the final 2:56. Their chants of "Defense, defense" could be described as nothing short of awe-inspiring.

BOB KNIGHT was responsible for those chants. A proud man, it had to be a courageous move for him to appeal to the crowd. After all, college coaches just don't do that sort of thing.

Winners do though, folks.

Thanks, Bob, for a very big thrill.

+++

DON'T misunderstand the preceding, sports fans. All was not roses at Assembly Hall Saturday.

Knight was so distressed by the turn of events following the game—Indiana's sub-par play and the crowd's near-silence for the

Knight's Cheerleading: A Really Great Moment

Great moments in sports come few and far between, and if you've been fortunate enough to see just one, you'll know what I mean when I say that such moments create a spine-tingling atmosphere and tend to leave a person feeling good allover.

I was in position to see even worse up close. Aiming a ball in my direction was a single instance, and now I would see another.

Knight's temper erupted after a disappointing defeat at Columbia, South Carolina, three days before Christmas in 1972—with me on the road trip.

The final score was 88-85. Particularly painful was the fact that the previously unbeaten Hoosiers (5-0) led by 10 at halftime, and by 16 in the second half.

In years since, I've referred to this loss as the Kevin Joyce game. Joyce brought his team back with phenomenal shooting (seven shots in a row at one point, most from long range). He stole the ball, he ran the floor, and he whipped a crowd of more than 12,000 into pandemonium as fans hovered courtside. Joyce finished with a season-high 41 points, 25 in the second half.

I was grateful to not have immediate access to the IU locker room afterward. There was an explosion going on inside that I could hear from the hallway. But I was on deadline, so I finally pleaded with a student manager to summon the coach.

To his credit, Knight appeared—a greatly agitated Knight. We (me and another reporter) joined him in a men's bathroom, the only convenient out-of-the-way location.

Knight was raging inside. He took out his pent-up anger by slamming metal partitions in the bathroom. It was madder than I'd ever seen him.

Yet he was somehow calm with his answers, even as I summoned courage to ask why he hadn't substituted veteran guards when Joyce couldn't be stopped.

Things worsened on the team plane. Knight loudly excoriated forward John Ritter for much of the flight home. He expected better leadership from the senior, holding him up as an example for others. Knight continued this tirade for what seemed like hours while the rest of us turned to duck and cover. No one else spoke.

Hurtful as this seemed, I believed it wasn't intended to be personal because Knight respected Ritter. The coach simply couldn't accept how his team lost and was taking steps to ensure it wouldn't happen that way again.

Games on the road were no different than those at home for Knight. I'd heard him say the court size wasn't different and the competition five-on-five regardless of venue. It mattered not the opponent or the score: respect for the game demanded the same focused effort. Knight's ability to successfully convey that to his players made him one of the winningest coaches in college basketball.

With the benefit of hindsight, the South Carolina loss was a significant step on that journey. But from my perspective, it was a troubling lesson.

South Carolina's rally was no fluke. Carolina had won 43 of its previous 47 games at home. Two weeks prior to hosting IU, Coach Frank McGuire's team had dominated Michigan State, 83-64.

History reminds us that Joyce, then a senior, became a first-round draft choice of the Golden State Warriors. His South Carolina teammates that night included a freshman, Alex English, later a high-scoring pro and member of the Naismith Memorial Basketball Hall of Fame; a junior, Brian Winters, another NBA first-round draft pick, and another freshman, Mike Dunleavy, who had a long NBA career as a player and coach. South Carolina ended the season with a 21-7 record, losing in the NCAA tournament to a Memphis State team that advanced to the Final Four.

It was a sign of Knight's coaching and Indiana's talent that the Hoosiers led well over half of the game. Downing and Ritter were skilled veterans who combined for 43 points. But three other first-year players were starting for IU: Steve Green (a sophomore who had not been eligible to play as a freshman), and freshmen Quinn Buckner and Jim Crews, who played because the "no freshmen" rule had been lifted.

Effective as the Hoosiers were for much of the game, the pressure of a zealous environment on young players took hold.

Despite the loss, or maybe because of it, Indiana's team improved over the course of the season and also reached the Final Four. More about that later.

But first, this. After what I saw in the bathroom interview and then heard on the plane, "Loyalty Royalty" began to wonder for the first time whether the coaching end justifies the means.

***

44

Loyalty Royalty? A fellow *Courier-Tribune* sportswriter stuck that tag on me because I often backed the Hoosiers as part of our weekly football predictions contest, even when they were underdogs. A look at my clips shows that I did get carried away at times in support of my alma mater.

So much for total objectivity. Then again, writing for a Bloomington newspaper, was that so wrong? We're covering the home team.

The answer, in hindsight, is that I tried my best and learned a lot, but I should have done better.

***

The '72-'73 season built to an amazing climax. After another loss (to Texas-El Paso) in a holiday tournament, the Hoosiers won eight in a row, dropped three of four, and then closed out the regular season with wins over Michigan State, Wisconsin, Iowa, and Purdue.

Cage Debut Showcases Benson, May

Players I covered are part of Hoosier basketball lore

The 57-55 victory over Wisconsin on February 24, 1973, produced one of the most dramatic scenes I covered as a sportswriter. It was a game that would be known forever as the "dead-asses" game.

This one qualified as a grinder. An eighth-place Wisconsin team kept things close at Assembly Hall as the Hoosiers shot terribly: .344 from the field and an exasperating 13-25 from the free-throw line. Every point seemed hard-won.

After 37 minutes of game time, a frustrated home crowd of 15,327 was barely murmuring. Then an Indiana player gave the kind of effort Knight demanded, and cherished. The player dove in an unsuccessful effort to save a loose ball, tumbling out of bounds. It was a terrific try, but the hustle drew barely a ripple from the stands. Indiana's home advantage had been lost in this low-scoring struggle; it was as if the seats were near-empty.

As the official signaled Wisconsin ball, a suddenly animated Knight leaped from his courtside seat. He'd seen enough. What happened next was a first-ever at Indiana, as far as I know.

Turning to the stands, the coach waved his arms almost frantically, as if trying to shove air upward. Knight beckoned fans to their feet, demanding recognition of his team's effort.

This was surprising, so much so that it took a few seconds for fans to catch on. Comprehending Knight's intent, they rose as one. A roar reached a crescendo and stayed that way until the final horn. It was so loud it was almost scary.

Booming chants of "defense, defense" poured forth. Indiana players were lifted to another level. Poor Wisconsin had trouble dribbling and passing in the din, let alone scoring. If a crowd ever deserved an assist, this was it.

"Knight's Cheerleading: A Really Great Moment," was the headline above my column.

His postgame press conference was anything but. Knight took no questions. Instead, he delivered a 148-word lecture and stormed out of the press room.

"I think it is an absolute crying shame," Knight said, "that 15,000 people can sit there on their dead asses at a ball game and a coach has to get up to get somebody to cheer." He said that given how well the team had played all season, it "is an absolute positive shame that 15,000 people can't give the team any more support than they gave out there today."

Indiana fans got the message. Hoosier hustle plays drew ovations from that game forward. Bob Knight made it so.

Assembly Hall is considered one of the most difficult places to play for opposing teams, when a pandemic hasn't closed the stands. This reputation took firm root because of the passionate display by a cheerleading coach, frustrated by so many "dead asses."

Upset as he seemed then, I now give him credit for a shrewd intent that produced desired results.

***

The man who could make even sportswriters blush (well, almost) intimidated Indiana crowds to the point where he controlled not only his team's behavior but the fans as well. When students began a "bullsh—" chant following questionable referee calls at another game, Knight made it clear to everyone that this sort of unsportsmanlike conduct wouldn't be tolerated at Assembly Hall. You may have heard that yell in other places, but not from an Indiana crowd with Knight on the sidelines. (If there was swearing, it came from him on the bench.)

Knight also established early on that his players should never be called for a technical foul. Those were his domain.

The 1972-73 season built to an amazing climax. The Hoosiers won the Big Ten, which meant that Knight was taking them to the NCAA tournament in just his second season as Indiana coach.

At the NCAA tourney, Indiana faced Marquette and another McGuire coach (Al, no relation to South Carolina's Frank) in the first round.

The very quotable and colorful Al McGuire would go on to win his own national title at Marquette in 1977. In 1973, his team included Maurice Lucas, who would become a solid NBA player, and Larry McNeill and Marcus Washington, who also were drafted by the pros.

But the steadily improving Hoosiers won, 75-69, at Nashville, Tennessee. Downing had 29 points and 10 rebounds while Lucas was limited to 12 and 5.

Indiana defeated rival Kentucky, 72-65, in the championship game of the Nashville regional. Downing again led all scorers with 23.

So we were on to St. Louis, and the Final Four.

***

I say "we," because Owens and I would represent the *C-T* on press row. Our hotel was the Chase Park Plaza, a downtown landmark that had served presidents of the United States, the Rolling Stones, Dean Martin, and other big names.

Heady stuff for a 23-year-old. As I entered the elevator, I heard "hold the door," so I did. Crowding in was Coach Rupp's Kentucky entourage, including "The Baron" himself. Another late night during our stay I found myself seated at the coffee shop with Al McGuire and evangelist Oral Roberts. Let it be remembered that the *Courier-Trib* scribe passed the ketchup to Oral Roberts.

After the win over Kentucky at Nashville, I had quoted the talented freshman, Buckner. "This is where we wanted to go from the start, babe," he gushed. "We're going to play UCLA!"

Be careful what you wish for. John Wooden's Bruins were on their way to their seventh consecutive national championship, their ninth in the last 10 years. And they were riding a *73-game* winning streak.

***

So, what's my greatest memory from UCLA's 70-59 victory that ended the Hoosiers' championship hopes?

49

I have a couple. First was the disappointment of falling behind, 40-22, at halftime. Had IU come this far to be just another lopsided victim of the Bruins?

The answer: no. From my seat (just behind the first row courtside) I had a clear view of Wooden. He had what looked like a game program rolled up in his hands. As Indiana mounted a stirring comeback, he kept rolling up that program. *Tighter. Tighter.* It must have seemed like a wet noodle when the Bruins finally regained momentum.

Hard-core Hoosier fans will remember this as the game where UCLA big man Bill Walton, saddled with four fouls, avoided his fifth when an apparent charging call against him turned into a call against Downing. That was Downing's fourth foul. When Steve fouled out soon after, he had scored more than half (26) of Indiana's 51 points.

Downing's final basket made the score UCLA 54, Indiana 51. The Hoosiers had outscored the Bruins by 29-14 in not quite 10 and a half minutes of playing time.

Knight called timeout when UCLA scored to turn the momentum. Then baskets by Ritter got Indiana within two points. But the balloon couldn't stay up without Downing. UCLA pulled away.

Downing outscored Walton for the game, 26-14, although Walton outrebounded him, 17-5.

In the second half, "We lost our poise for the first time this year," Wooden admitted.

***

My memory of Bob Knight after the loss? Calm, professional, gracious. He didn't dispute the controversial foul, focusing instead on the crevasse Indiana fell into by halftime.

IU's trustees awarded him a five-year contract extension the next day, a Friday. That squelched rumors he might be lured away.

Knight's team still had a game to play at St. Louis. Indiana cruised to victory over Providence for third place (consolation games have long since been axed).

I have many reasons for being grateful to that Indiana team for getting me to my first (and only) Final Four. One was my chance to cover the championship game when UCLA routed Memphis State. Walton played one of the greatest games in NCAA history, scoring 44 points (including 21 of 22 field goals).

***

Attention pulls like a magnet toward a program reaching the national spotlight, and that was true for covering Knight's Hoosiers. Every move of note in the off-season drew coverage, including one of the biggest recruiting gets in school history, 6-11 center Kent Benson from New Castle, Indiana. Benson chose IU over Kentucky and Notre Dame.

So now the 1973-74 Hoosiers would add not only Benson but Scott May and Bobby Wilkerson, two very talented players who were ineligible as freshmen for academic reasons. All would eventually become starters for a team returning Green, Buckner, Crews and super-sub John Laskowski.

The Bob Knight I knew was a man who frequently did nice things for people. I saw that at a preseason practice game scheduled at Jeffersonville, Indiana. Knight took along Ernie Andres, a Jeffersonville native who had been a good IU basketball player and the school's longtime baseball coach. Knight also took Ritter, the graduated senior who bought into Knight's disciplined approach and seemed to drain every ounce of effort from his body. "John may not be the smartest player in the world," Knight once said, "but he ranks among the top two or three."

Knight made a point of introducing Andres and Ritter to the Jeffersonville crowd.

Another thing that impressed me in covering Knight's teams was how he would almost always find a way to praise a player for setting a good screen, throwing an alert pass, or making a particularly good defensive play. Often that praise went to a substitute who played only a few minutes. Meanwhile, leading scorers often drew merely equivalent praise—if that—from the man who spent most of his Ohio State career coming off the bench.

The not-so-subtle message: Value the little things, because they are instrumental to team success.

***

The Knight I knew never seemed impressed by professional basketball and its often casual approach to defense. I'm not sure how many NBA games he's seen in person over the years, but my guess is darn few.

An exception came in the fall of 1973, at an *exhibition* game, no less. Knight was in the stands when Downing

52

(a first-round draft choice of the Boston Celtics) returned to Indianapolis to face the Pacers.

The message, again hardly subtle: If you made it through his demanding classroom and showed him your loyalty, you got it right back.

***

When the next season began in December of '73. I had no idea that my full-time sports writing career wouldn't last the month.

Two days after Christmas, *C-T* staffers learned they had published the final issue of the newspaper. The business side wasn't pulling in enough revenue, so we were an early casualty in the demise of many newspapers.

I wrote stories and columns about the six games scheduled between December 1 and 22. "Knight's Strategy: Stroke of Genius" was the headline above a column about Indiana's 77-68 win over Kentucky at Louisville. Trailing by five points at halftime, Knight adjusted his defense, got the lead, and then had the Hoosiers play keep-away for the final nine minutes of the game (no shot clock back then). Indiana posted an almost unheard of .818 from the field in the last half, feasting on layups and holding Kentucky to 32 percent.

Irony of ironies, my final coverage for the *Courier-Tribune* came three days before Christmas at Assembly Hall, when IU hosted a return match with South Carolina. Indiana won, 84-71. Knight visited the losers' dressing room after the game to wish them well. What a difference from a year earlier.

***

Indiana was playing in the Far West Classic at Portland, Oregon, the day the presses stopped for the last time for the *C-T*. Bob Owens made the road trip, covering Far West games in our final issue.

I was among the lucky ones who quickly found a new job. In the next few days, I landed a reporting slot in newswriting with the state's largest newspaper, *The Indianapolis Star*. I was hired to fill a one-person news bureau in West Lafayette, Indiana, of all places. (The location of Indiana's greatest rival, Purdue.)

Transitioning to a new job kept me from saying goodbye to Knight and the players I'd covered and interviewed.

But it wasn't my last interaction with the coach.

***

It's strange to go from "no cheering in the press box" to being able to root for Knight's Hoosiers. And even stranger to do it from West Lafayette.

At this point, I should say that I'd been rooting for IU sports teams since my dad moved our family from Colorado to Indiana in the 1960s. I planned to attend Indiana University and its journalism school once it became apparent that becoming a reporter was my goal.

In college I was selected sports editor of *The Indiana Daily Student*, later vying for editor-in-chief. When I wasn't selected, I left the *Daily Student* for the *C-T* while wrapping up my senior year.

In addition to the *C-T*, I made a few bucks phoning in IU scores and stats to United Press International. UPI's sports editor asked me to continue that job for Purdue football and basketball. This allowed me to keep my hand in, sports-wise.

A year passed. Following the Hoosiers on TV, it was obvious that Knight had a great chance to get IU back to the NCAA tourney. His '73-'74 team had just missed the big dance, losing a Big Ten championship playoff game to Michigan.

By now Scott May, Kent Benson, Quinn Buckner, Steve Green, Laskowski, and Bobby Wilkerson were well known to college basketball fans across the country. And all of them were returning to play in '74-75.

From my apartment in West Lafayette, I watched IU games on Indianapolis-based Channel 4, or sometimes national telecasts. I listened as Knight recapped win after win on his Channel 4-based Bob Knight Show, serving up strategic insights I'd never heard from other coaches. Credit host Chuck Marlowe for his stiff hide on that show, because the coach often showed impatience toward him. (Some have called Chuck "Knight's punching bag." Marlowe died at 86 in 2016.)

By year-end 1974, the team was 11-0 and had dominated all but one opponent, winning by double figures except for an overtime escape at Kansas. Thrashings included 94-74 over Kentucky, 97-60 over Nebraska, and 102-71 over Ohio State at the Rainbow Classic in Hawaii.

I wrote a letter to Knight, congratulating him on the success. He responded on January 14, 1975, thanking me for writing. "If you get a chance to come down, don't hesitate to give me a call," he wrote, adding that he greatly appreciated hearing from me. He also wrote this:

"The team has been doing well in most games, but there are some things we need to improve."

That sentence pretty much sums up Bob Knight's standard of excellence. His letter was dated the day after IU improved to 15-0 by overwhelming Minnesota, 79-59.

***

This particular Knight team meant a lot to me personally, for reasons the coach never knew. Steve Green, his first recruit at Indiana, was the son of Ray Green, a fine gentleman and briefly the head coach at my high school.

Ray Green knew I liked sports, so I was appointed statistician for his Frankfort team. He had me gather clippings about upcoming opponents, conferring as if my opinion mattered. Ray was a fine man.

Ray had three tall sons, including Steve, who played for their dad when Ray left Frankfort for Silver Creek in southern Indiana. Thanks to my role for UPI, I was in the press area at Purdue's Mackey Arena when Steve excelled as Indiana visited for a game on February 22, 1975.

If you've never been to Mackey, it's a round arena that reverberates noise such that some fans bring earplugs. My dad took brother David and me to its dedication game when I was in high school, a thriller matching Purdue and Rick Mount against UCLA and Lew (later to become Kareem Abdul-Jabbar) Alcindor.

Loud as that was, the sound didn't compare to this Purdue-Indiana game. Indiana was unbeaten with 23 wins at that point, and had routed Purdue at Bloomington, 104-71. Payback was in the air.

The Hoosiers came out strong, and Green was amazing. His outside shot was so good it hardly touched the rim. He led IU to a 50-point first half. But, uh-oh, Purdue had 46.

Back and forth it went, a game where Green scored 29 points. In a brilliant shooting display, he hit 13 of 15 field goals, says the Hoosier press guide. My scorebook had him 13-14, his only miss a layup.

With Indiana leading by a point as the clock ran down, Buckner and Wilkerson combined to knock the ball away from Purdue and down to the other end of the floor. I remember Knight exulting (rare for him). He had his first-ever win at Mackey, 83-82.

The arena had been silenced by the Hoosiers, now 24-0. But exciting as things were in the moment, something else happened that day to mar the record for perhaps Knight's best-ever team.

***

It seems strange to say that Indiana in 1974-75 could have been Knight's best squad, given that his IU teams won the national title the next year and in 1981 and 1987.

The '74-75 team had not only all of the players who would start for the 1976 national champions, but also Green and Laskowski. Few college teams have ever been so deep and talented.

There was so much talent on the '74-'75 team, it would be difficult to name a "best player." Wilkerson was tall, long, and quick and excelled defensively. Buckner, who came to Indiana as both a football and basketball player, was an incredible competitor and quarterback on the floor. Benson was terrific in the post. Then you also had Green, Laz, and Tom Abernethy....

....And Scott May. May, a sharpshooting forward, had led IU in scoring in nearly half the games (12 of 25) heading to West Lafayette. But at some point in the Purdue game (I can't recall exactly when), he walked off the floor, holding his left arm. It was fractured. Indiana beat Purdue even though he was limited to 8 points.

May missed the next two games, appearing briefly in the final two games of the unbeaten regular season (30-0). IU was sent to Dayton, Ohio, for the then 32-team NCAA tournament. May came off the bench but didn't score as the Hoosiers won their first-round game over Oregon State behind another great night from Steve Green, 34 points.

What happened next at Dayton—March 22, 1975—was grim, almost death-in-the-family grim for me and so many other fans of that team. Knight started Scott May against Kentucky. May gamely tried to play with a cast but struggled against a tall Kentucky team that had greatly improved since Indiana trounced the Wildcats, 98-74, in December.

Scott May had scored 25 points in that December victory. At Dayton, he managed just 2 points, shooting 1 for 4 from the field. And Kentucky defeated IU, 92-90.

***

I was only able to watch from afar the next season when the Hoosiers celebrated a 32-0 record and their first national championship under Knight.

A healthy Scott May averaged 23.5 points and was a unanimous first-team All-American and Collegiate Player of the Year.

May, Buckner, Wilkerson, and Abernethy graduated, leaving Benson as the only returning starter for the '76-'77 team. Understandably, it was a much more difficult season. Teams that had been thumped by the Hoosiers for several years exacted revenge. Indiana slipped from 32-0 to 14-13.

From my perch in the Purdue press area, I watched Benson wheeled off the floor after he took a hard fall in a game won by the Boilermakers, 86-78.

Losing was tough on fans accustomed to winning. When IU rebounded to 21-8 the next year, advancing once again to the NCAA tournament, things looked rosy once again.

But Bob Knight made a significant change, one that I was disappointed to learn.

***

In late 1977, I read that Knight had decided to no longer speak to reporters in postgame news conferences. This followed skirmishes with the news media. He still had reporters he trusted, some good friends. But the rest were now shut out.

This was contrary to the Knight I knew, who saw it as his obligation to meet with reporters—even in circumstances like the loss at South Carolina.

So I wrote another letter, dated December 29, 1977. The previous evening I had watched the telecast of the Gator Bowl Championship game in which IU beat Florida, 73-60.

"The way the Hoosiers scrapped reminded me of the Green-Downing-Ritter-Buckner etc. club I was privileged to cover years ago," I wrote before getting to the reason for the letter.

"This regards your policy of not speaking to reporters after games. I realize you have your own reason for this, undoubtedly a good and sensible one. But it bothers me somewhat, nevertheless."

I went on to explain that with his talents at the top of the profession, "only you can give the best insight as to this style of coaching....you are most qualified to comment on Indiana's basketball successes and failures."

I told him that he was depriving Hoosier fans of his insights. "One might argue that difficulties with reporters involving accuracy or editorial bias is sufficient reason to discontinue talking to all reporters. But I hate to see that happen. I remember being a young reporter who had some difficulty communicating at times with a young coach, but neither of us let that stand in the way of getting the job done. I know I learned much from the experience, and I'm just dumb enough to think there were thousands of people out there who ate up every word of every interview concerning IU basketball at the time."

Indiana defeated Iowa on January 5, 1978. In a letter dated the next day, Knight responded:

"Many thanks for taking the time to drop me a note. I greatly appreciate your thoughtfulness in doing so as well as your thoughts on the press. I have made some changes in a number of things relative to the use of my time, with the press only being a part of the overall picture. What I have done has been a result of a lot of thought on what I think is best for our basketball program. However, I do appreciate what you had to say."

The Bob Knight I Knew

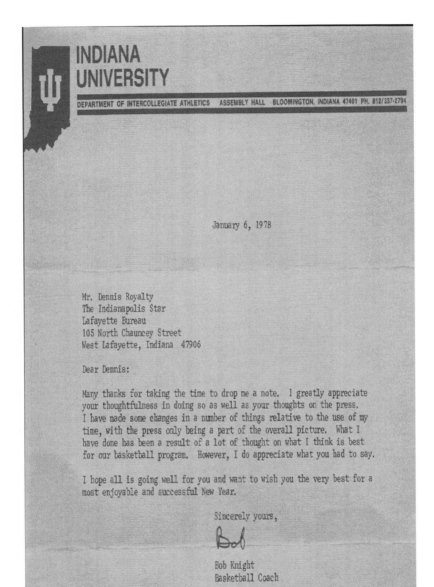

INDIANA UNIVERSITY

DEPARTMENT OF INTERCOLLEGIATE ATHLETICS   ASSEMBLY HALL   BLOOMINGTON, INDIANA 47401 PH. 812/337-2794

January 6, 1978

Mr. Dennis Royalty
The Indianapolis Star
Lafayette Bureau
105 North Chauncey Street
West Lafayette, Indiana 47906

Dear Dennis:

Many thanks for taking the time to drop me a note. I greatly appreciate
your thoughtfulness in doing so as well as your thoughts on the press.
I have made some changes in a number of things relative to the use of my
time, with the press only being a part of the overall picture. What I
have done has been a result of a lot of thought on what I think is best
for our basketball program. However, I do appreciate what you had to say.

I hope all is going well for you and want to wish you the very best for a
most enjoyable and successful New Year.

Sincerely yours,

Bob Knight
Basketball Coach

A courteous but disappointing letter from the coach

***

Again, the response was a disappointment. It also was my last communication with the coach. My life changed dramatically over the next few years, as I married Ginger and we were blessed with son Andrew and daughter Kelsey. In 1982, I was promoted to city editor at *The Star*, responsible for a staff of more than 50.

***

I made time to follow the Hoosiers closely, celebrating national championships in 1981 and 1987 and watching as Knight coached the USA team to a gold medal in 1984, and was inducted into the National Collegiate Basketball Hall of Fame in 1991.

He didn't notice, but I was seated with family not far from his team's bench at Frankfort in 1992 during filming of the movie *"Blue Chips."* Nick Nolte's portrayal of Coach Pete Bell had many similarities to Knight, but one thing Knight did not have in common with the fictional coach was cheating to lure top recruits. Knight was not a rule-breaker and, in that respect, should always be hailed as a role model.

In other respects, however, he had become anything but. Coach Knight could be rude, crude, disrespectful, and at times so ugly in public behaviors I was ashamed for him.

How could a man lose his temper to the point where he would throw a chair during a Purdue game, or angrily lay his hands on Neil Reed at practice, prompting a firestorm of controversy and outrage?

Reed, for heaven's sake, was a player who gave Knight everything he had.

How do you explain the coaching excesses reported by John Feinstein, author of the best-selling "*A Season on the Brink*"?

These are but a sampling of the things that stained a coaching icon and cost him his job at IU.

***

I tried to make sense of all this for readers on May 23, 2000. I was then chief of a news bureau for *The Star*, and wrote a weekly column.

Knight had recently been disciplined by IU President Myles Brand, who warned that there was now a zero-tolerance policy for poor conduct. As it turned out, this was Brand's last step before firing the coach.

In my column, I mentioned the relationship of mutual respect I'd had with Knight. I then lamented what his behaviors had caused.

"I believe his only hope of surviving IU's zero-tolerance mandate is to start caring about other people again: his players, his family, fishing buddies, and the rest of us—secretaries, athletic directors, even those in the media who dare to disagree with him. He should treat others as he'd like to be treated himself."

Alas, Knight didn't or wouldn't understand. This from a well-read man who not only changed the way the college game was played in the 1970s, but was a vigorous supporter of the IU library, and, as I've said, a man who could do incredibly nice things.

One of those was helping Bob Owens find work after the *Courier-Tribune* folded. I tried to confirm this myself, unsuccessfully. But in Laskowski's book, *"Tales from the Hoosiers Locker Room,"* he reveals that Knight first used his contacts to help Owens land a job in Lincoln, Nebraska. And he did it again when that newspaper also went under, helping Bob find work at *The Columbus Dispatch* in Ohio. Laskowski also reported that Knight helped pay medical expenses for Max Stultz, a sportswriter for *The Indianapolis Star*, when Stultz suffered a serious illness.

Many of Knight's former players not only remain loyal to him, but love him. So do thousands if not tens of thousands of fans who flocked to his speaking engagements and appreciated his final coaching years at Texas Tech.

As for the coach himself, here are telling quotes from a *Chicago Tribune* article I found online. Staff Writer Skip Myslenski had interviewed Knight in a story that also appeared in May of 2000.

Knight told Myslenski that people would remember two things of his time at Indiana. One was that he was honest. The second? "I can't mold myself to what other people want me to be … There has to be in each one of us, in order to be successful, a willingness not just to accept those things that we feel are inadequate, but to do something about them. That is often misconstrued as temperament.

"I've always felt that it is necessary, when trying to reach a particular end, to be emphatic about the means that are to be used to reach that end."

***

To that point, coach, it's a matter of how emphatic. Too much so is where we part ways.

What is it about exceptional people that can, for some, lead to erratic or surprisingly objectionable behavior? I have no answer. What I do know is I was privileged to watch up close as one of the greatest strategists in the game's history practiced his craft.

The Bob Knight I knew did expose his temper, but largely in private surroundings, like practice. His coaching style was strategic, I believed—designed so his charges would "play to their potential."

The Bob Knight I knew was a man who would apologize for his excesses.

How I wish the Bob Knight I knew could have left the school I loved on good terms, respected by all. It was nice to see him finally return to Assembly Hall. Congratulations to former players for making that happen and for their love and loyalty to him.

If only everyone could still feel that way.

Writing Tip #5—Fact-Check Relentlessly

You are singularly responsible for the accuracy of your story or book.

Writing *"The Bob Knight I Knew"* reminded me of a mistake I made as a young reporter. It's a mistake you'll avoid if you follow this rule:

Never take someone else's word for information that should be double-checked.

Here's why: I covered a particularly thrilling IU win when, after the game, I spotted Bob's wife (first wife) who was ecstatic. I did a quick interview and decided to quote her in my column.

Except for one thing: while I recognized who she was, we hadn't met and I forgot to ask her name.

On deadline, I turned to the sports editor to ask if he knew. "Betty," he shot back confidently. No hesitation, no doubt. So I wrote Betty.

Which would have been fine if her name wasn't Nancy.

I phoned to apologize when someone who knew Nancy read the column and contacted me. Nancy and the coach were forgiving and appreciative that I called.

(I've wondered since if they would have been as generous had I made the mistake after a crushing defeat.)

No matter. I blew it.

So learn from this: check facts yourself so you always have firsthand knowledge of what you write. There are no shortcuts to accuracy for writers who want to be trusted and respected.

One more thing: if you make mistakes, own up to them. To not do so damages credibility even more.

The 39 Bars

Arm strength has never been my strength, as you'll recall from my funnel-breaking episode in Chapter 1.

Running? Jumping? I've managed those. Back in 1972 at Army Basic Training, I tackled the merciless hills of Fort Knox, Kentucky, while lugging a heavy backpack. There's good reason why those elevations are nicknamed Misery, Agony, and Heartbreak. Some soldiers-in-training fell out of line marching them, but not me.

I also conquered the mile run in under eight minutes wearing clunky Army boots.

I survived those rituals and plenty more at Fort Knox, and became a better man because of it.

But one military test haunted me. It involved pulling myself down a row of monkey bars, one at a time for 39 reps. Trainees can't leave active duty training without accomplishing the feat.

Technically, though, I didn't.

Or did I?

***

This story is about the 39-bar episode. However, it begins with another number: 119.

Number 119 is why I wound up at the Fort Knox U.S. Army Training Center.

My college years at Indiana University (1967-71) coincided with the worst casualties of the Vietnam War. In '68 alone, 16,592 members of the U.S. Armed Forces died of wounds suffered nearly 14,000 miles away. Another 11,616 died the next year, 1969.

IU was one of many campuses embroiled in war protests. Marchers jammed the streets bearing peace signs and angry slogans. When antiwar presidential candidate Eugene McCarthy came to speak, students filled pretty Dunn Meadow. (It helped that Peter, Paul and Mary and other music acts accompanied McCarthy.)

Those were intense, bewildering times. In 1970 at the *Indiana Daily Student* newspaper, I watched a wire service machine clatter terrible news of students mowed down by the Ohio National Guard. Most Kent State demonstrators were close in age to soldiers losing their lives in huge numbers overseas.

Would this nightmare ever end?

Our government conducted a lottery in December 1969 to ensure adequate stocking of the armed services pipeline. Birth dates were plucked at random to determine which men would serve.

My 1949 birth date made me lottery-eligible as part of a group born between 1944 and 1950.

It wasn't certain how many of us would be needed. Estimates were that the first 150 to 175 numbers selected in the lottery should fill needed troop strength.

The first date picked at random (number 1) was September 14, meaning that men born on that date were certain to be drafted. Number 366 was June 8th (leap years included).

Lottery coverage in *The Indiana Daily Student* featured interviews with several male students who were part of the lottery pool. One, born June 8, provided the best quote: "My talent for being last finally paid off."

My birthday, September 23, became lottery number 119. This ensured that the draft would extend to me.

Which meant a personal dilemma.

***

I had a conservative upbringing that honored military service. My dad was a veteran of the Army Air Corps; his father and a cousin joined the Navy. On my mother's side, another cousin served in Vietnam.

I never participated in war protests. Training to become a journalist, I was determined to maintain objectivity.

My neutrality was such that I fussed when an assistant professor told our class he could no longer teach in good conscience while war continued. The teacher compromised with me, agreeing to continue classes but only outdoors. (Why that made a difference to him, I can't recall. I do remember classmates wishing that I'd kept my mouth shut.)

I confess to having serious doubts about the war. I kept those views within my friendship circle.

A college deferment meant that I wouldn't be drafted until after graduation in May 1971. My parents feared for my life as that time approached, regardless of their feelings about the war. So did other friends. But what to do?

Someone suggested I try enlisting in the National Guard unit headquartered in my college town, Bloomington. That seemed a good compromise. At the time, Guard units weren't routinely called for active duty.

I wasn't optimistic about being accepted. Surely, thousands of others had the same idea and the Guard would be at full strength. Instead, I found Sgt. Walt Conner not only welcoming but in need of a personnel clerk. I agreed to a six-year hitch that included monthly meetings, two-week summer obligations, and, of course, 120 days of active duty training.

Then came another break. My active duty training would take place at Fort Knox, fewer than three hours from Bloomington.

***

My Basic Training outfit was Company B, 7th Battalion, 2nd Brigade, First U.S. Army. Some were also Guard enlistees, but most in Company B were regular U.S. Army. We arrived from different places with different races, accents, and educational levels. I was assigned a bunkmate who, it turned out, couldn't read letters from his girlfriend. I read them to him.

A trainee's experience begins at something called the reception station. This is your introduction to being addressed as less than human. Two or three days are spent collecting Army gear, getting your hair sheared, and learning to snap to attention.

Our sergeant at the reception station was a tough guy, experienced at breaking down individual will in service to the Army mindset.

Still, I did have a nice experience at the reception station, a brief uplifting moment in a period of apprehension.

The sergeant summoned me outside the barracks. Thinking the worst, I was instead greeted by a friendly face—Lt. Rich Honack, an IU friend. I had no idea that Honack was assigned to Fort Knox, or that he'd enlisted.

Honack had spotted my name on the reception station roster, so he decided to visit me. We chatted cordially while the sergeant had to maintain an "at ease" posture, doing his best to hide aggravation and listen patiently as Honack asked how I was doing.

Score one for the little guy.

Dispatched to my Basic Training unit, life consisted of little sleep, strenuous physical activity, and learning the expectations of a soldier. Our drill sergeant made the guy at the reception station seem angelic. Pity the poor trainee who overlooked a spot of dust on his M16A1 rifle.

We crawled through mud on our bellies, inching beneath barbed wire while bullets whizzed overhead. We pulled KP duty, force-marched up and down those blasted hills, and endured overnight bivouac in freezing weather.

It wasn't easy to cope with the mental side, notably the copious harassment. Labeled "college boy," I got more than my share. As time went on and we accustomed ourselves to instinctive military responses, the sergeant backed off a tad. He made me a squad leader and, on rare instances, even tolerated my joking with him.

By the tenth and final week, it was clear that this career drill sergeant had only done what he was asked to do: prepare men for life-threatening times that loomed ahead for most.

I look back on those 10 weeks as exasperating and humiliating. But the experience also was exhilarating and self-affirming when you realize, "I can take what you're throwing at me." You swell with pride while proving yours is the best training unit, or when saluting the flag while in uniform.

***

Graduation from Basic leads to further training in your area of specialization. Personnel specialist training would complete my 120 days of active duty.

By now I'd lost nearly 30 pounds. Those pounds stayed off, since significant PT (physical training) accompanied clerk schooling.

Leaving Advanced Individual Training after 120 days would be contingent on successfully completing not only clerk training but also passing a six-item PT test.

All that seemed easy. Except for one thing: achieving 39 repetitions by hauling oneself down the horizontal bars.

This was no big deal for those with strong arms and good coordination. Not for me, though.

A trip down the monkey bars requires progressing along an elevated sideways ladder, positioned 10 feet or so in the air. One length of the apparatus covers 11 bars.

Once you've reached the end of them for the first time, you must do a 180-degree turn, head back the other way for 11 more rungs (22 total), do it again (to 33), and, finally, down the bars once more until the 39th.

My 120th day of advanced training was scheduled for completion on April 5, 1972, a Wednesday. As bad luck would have it, the bars were the final part of the PT test, administered a few days before April 5.

Recognizing that I had barely made 11 bars before falling off in a run-through at the start of clerk school, I had work to do. I was determined to pass the PT test and return home (as scheduled) to a newspaper job I'd taken in Bloomington.

So, for a couple of weeks, I charged out of the mess hall after supper to practice, practice, practice on the bars.

I'd watched others closely as to how this was done. I learned that arm strength is just a part of this exercise; coordinated movement is crucial. Smaller guys seem to pull it off easily as if dancing in air. It's not that I'm so much taller (6-feet), but rather this type of coordination has always been difficult for me.

Resolved to improve, I laid in a plan to repeat on every attempt:

After climbing to bar level, reach for the first rung. Let your body swing forward, grasping the bar only momentarily with one hand. Swing!

Maintain forward momentum without pausing. Don't spend much time hanging onto any one bar; instead, establish a rhythm, swinging forward. Let weight work in your favor, not against.

*Keep swinging, dammit! At the end of the row, let your weight swing briefly away from the apparatus. As gravity swings you back toward the bars, quickly change hands while spinning around, letting body weight force you to the opposite direction. Sustain momentum, hand over hand, one rung at a time, don't look down, stare ahead, make the turn again, and again, keep going....**don't fall before 39!***

Night after night I performed this routine, alone, determined to defeat my white whale. Pleasant spring weather helped. I improved from making just one trip down the bars to two, then three. Then, eureka! All the way to 50.

I was ready. My departure on the 120th day of training was all but assured.

***

Ugh. Then came an unwelcome surprise.

Overnight before the PT test, temperatures plunged. The bars were ice cold at 8 a.m.

Dozens of us were lined up behind six or seven sets of bars, with examiners posted to grade us. Waiting in line, I noticed that only some trainees were managing to reach the 39-bar requirement. Frosty rungs had become slippery after being smeared by the first round of trainees.

Trainees who had buzzed through the exercise on days when conditions were ideal now struggled or slipped off early. And this was a pass or fail test, with no second chances.

Watching in line, my confidence ebbed. Rocking back and forth in the cold, I repeated my silent practice mantra. When my turn came, I seized the forward momentum I'd hoped for down the first row, then slipped, recovered, lost my balance, recovered, made a second turn, slipped, lost forward momentum, tried to regain it…

…And fell.

I'd made it beyond 22 bars, but not close to the magic 39. My examiner failed me. I was crushed.

Disappointment was compounded by consternation when I returned to the barracks and learned that many of my pals who also didn't make the full 39 received passing grades anyway.

At this point, dear reader, you may wonder, what's the big deal? It was for me. Another PT test wasn't scheduled for nearly two weeks, beyond my 120th end date. I'd promised myself and my employer that I would be back to work. More than that, I had so looked forward to ending training that was successfully completed in all other respects.

***

Let me add a truth I had observed about the Army when I was in training. Some Fort Knox staff members looked the other way to accommodate trainees. (Cheating, in other words).

Example: After a few practice rounds in Basic Training, I passed the rifle test even though this was the first place I'd ever fired a gun. Yet others were given passing marks despite some pretty lousy shooting.

Worse, I saw a sharpshooting candidate from Tennessee pass the test for other trainees while graders looked on.

Similarly, at the bars exercise, some examiners marked candidates "completed" when that wasn't true on a very cold day in late March 1972. Friends in the barracks confirmed it for me.

I explained this to my sergeant when I asked to see him the day after the bars test. I told him that conditions marred the test for many of us.

The sergeant was unsympathetic. "You failed and you admit you failed," he said. "I'm sorry we'll be keeping you past 120 days, but that's the way it goes."

I volunteered to follow him to the bars to give me another chance. He said no, that testing only occurred as scheduled.

So, I steeled myself, took a deep breath, and said, "I'd like to speak to the captain."

***

Pursuing chain of command in the military is a little like the prime directive in *"Star Trek."* You abide by it.

My sergeant wasn't happy, but he scheduled time for me with the captain on my 119th day at Fort Knox.

A lowly PFC (private first class) seldom interacts with a captain. But I wasn't intimidated. I was a reporter, a business-journalism graduate who had interviewed Senator Birch Bayh and Coach Bob Knight. What did I have to lose?

I felt cheated and motivated to get back to life and work in Bloomington. I was the victim of circumstances since others who shouldn't have passed were moving on.

The captain was courteous but unyielding. "You have a record of incompletion," he said. "There's nothing I can do."

While unmoved by my pleading, he did seem to take note of what I'd said about the unethical examiners.

I told him that I appreciated his willingness to see me.

And then I respectfully asked to appeal his decision to the brigade colonel.

***

This was a "Say what?" moment. But I was serious. All my life I'd been told to stand up for what I believed. My dad, a personnel manager, often was the arbiter of workplace disputes and stressed the importance of following the chain of command.

I felt it was my duty not only to stick up for myself but to let the colonel know what I'd seen.

"Report back here at 8 hundred hours," the captain snapped, displeased. He was aware that Saturday was my 120th day.

So I did report to the command office on my 120th day of active duty. I arrived early and was met by a soldier who was aware of my appointment.

"Royalty, you have two choices," he said.

Two choices?

"You can see the colonel. Or, you can take your completed paperwork and be released to your Guard unit."

I did an about-face, gathered my things, and drove north to civilian life.

***

Postscript: As I write this, it's been 43 years since I was honorably discharged after six years of National Guard service in artillery units at Bloomington and Lebanon, Indiana. Some memories of Fort Knox remain fresh. They include sitting in a circle on grass while sergeants read where trainees would report to their next assignments.

I knew I would remain at Fort Knox for clerk school. No suspense for me. I joined others in a sarcastic cheer when one lucky fellow was announced as heading to Hawaii for radio school. But there was noticeable quiet when so many trainees learned they were headed to combat training, the next step before Southeast Asia.

Over the decades I've been reluctant to stand when attending concerts or other events where veterans were asked to be recognized. Yes, I served. But I didn't put my life on the line for my country as they did. My Guard unit could have been activated, but it wasn't.

I've wondered what happened to my Fort Knox comrades who served in Nam. I'm grateful for your service, men, and glad I spent time alongside you.

Writing Tip #6—Drawing them out.

The best interviewers avoid yes or no questions, listen carefully, pose follow-up questions, and seek clarification when in doubt.

I've interviewed rich and poor, convicts and celebrities, governors and senators, relatives reeling from tragedy, and people accused of wrongdoing who were leery of sharing anything with a reporter.

In each case, preparation is essential for the successful interviewer, as I noted in Advice #3.

Here are recommendations for how best to draw out subjects during the actual interview:

State your purpose in advance. Some investigative reporters avoid this, preferring "an ambush" interview. My feeling is that a writer who asks for honesty should approach with honesty. It's best to be straightforward with your interview subject.

Conduct the interview in person. Phone interviewing sometimes is unavoidable due to timing and travel distance, but if you have a choice, in-person interviews are best. It's not only the most comfortable choice for your subject, but it offers a chance to observe and learn more about the person **and** the story. This can lead to icebreaking questions and even fodder for what you write.

Create a constructive atmosphere with your opening questions, but don't dawdle. Respect the subject's time.

Solicit telling responses by avoiding yes or no questions. Questions like, "Can you give me an example? Or, "How did that work for you?" draw out the subject.

Listen, listen, listen. Follow-up when insights are shared that will most benefit your audience.

In asking difficult questions, consider this approach that I've used successfully: "A skeptic might say you were motivated by self-interest when you did that," or, "Will the average person think what you did was the best way to proceed?" This is an honest way of framing questions that often results in the most telling responses.

If interviewing someone in grief, tread lightly at the outset. Begin with factual questions, such as the age of a loved one, a place of birth, number of brothers and sisters, and so forth. This helps the subject focus and creates trust because it's clear you care about accuracy.

End the interview with "What have I forgotten?" or "What else do you think I should know before we wrap up?" Many times this question led to the heart of my stories. Subjects appreciate being asked and often are so comfortable by that point in an interview, he or she is ready to share information candidly.

Finally, don't be afraid to contact the subject for follow-up later if you aren't clear about something once you begin writing. This is not only respectful but necessary in the pursuit of accuracy and truth.

Finding Karen

Karen Stotts, you were just 17. I was 24. In the more than 45 years since our paths crossed at tornado-ravaged Monticello, I've wondered about your life. You endured so much.

***

It was April 3, 1974. I was a rookie news reporter based in West Lafayette, Indiana. Notice I said "news" reporter. When *The Indianapolis Star* hired me that January, my hard news experience was minimal. I'd spent most of the previous three years covering sports for a paper that folded.

The Star assigned me to a one-person bureau in West Lafayette, churning out news of northern Indiana. These were short items, mostly. Things like faculty raises granted at Purdue University, traffic fatalities, and so forth. Break-in stuff.

But April 3 was different. Ominous. Not a day for routine reporting.

It was raining hard, faucet-raining hard. Tornado warnings, too. So I phoned my boss in downtown Indianapolis, State Editor Ernie Wilkinson.

"Denny, this looks real bad. Better get to the state police post."

Understandable. The West Lafayette State Police Post was the emergency nerve center for a dozen counties. I got drenched scrambling from my Chevelle to the door of the post. Roaring winds made an umbrella useless. Not only that, it was dark outside, twilight-like. Odd for

3:30 p.m. Inside the post, activity swirled. Police radios chattered and pointed troopers to calls for help. This was no drill. I found a phone and called Ernie. He was about to send me to one of the most jarring experiences of my life.

***

Ernest A. Wilkinson was a devoted, passionate newsman. By the time I worked for him in '74, he was 49 and had been state editor for Indiana's largest newspaper for 14 years. On the way up, he'd chased hundreds if not thousands of deadline stories.

Breaking news was Ernie's lifeblood. Now on his desk were reports of a massive tornado outbreak.

Ernie knew that Rainsville, a tiny community near the state's western border, was being torn apart. That tornado originated in Illinois and was rampaging through his territory.

Ernie also realized that from his experience, most tornadoes travel from southwest to northeast. And 65 miles from where he was sitting, he had a reporter near a likely path.

Me.

***

Ernie guessed where this powerful storm was heading. He laid a ruler across the state map he knew almost by heart. He was searching for the most populated area on the frightening route.

"Denny, head for Monticello. Call from there."

I remember no other conversation at the state police post, where troopers were overwhelmed by a ringing

84

switchboard. So it was back to my Chevelle, back to chase a tornado, an excited 24-year-old handed a major story.

Danger didn't occur. It was sometime around 4:30 p.m.

***

Monticello, Indiana, population 5,000-plus, is the White County seat, hugging the Tippecanoe River. A 40-50 minute drive should get me there.

Emerging from the furious rainstorm, I learned through radio static that this looked to be a major outbreak. So be alert, be ready to take cover.

Still, I saw little evidence of tornado-like weather. Neck-craning toward a brighter sky, I saw only clouds sailing at a rapid clip.

Maybe halfway there, the sky turned an eerie green. And yet it was calm as I approached Monticello. The time was about 5:30 p.m.

***

On the outskirts, a curiosity. A few cars had parked right in the traffic lane, where the highway became a city street. They'd stopped without regard for anyone behind. There were no drivers or passengers in sight.

I soon found out why. Parking off the pavement at the edge of Monticello, I walked into a nightmare.

Huge trees had uprooted, many resting on rooftops or ripped through them. Debris littered neighborhood yards and streets, including downed power lines.

Now I knew why it was impossible to drive further into the city.

I saw cars overturned and others shoved into front yards, where they plowed deep gashes into lawns. The few people I saw wore dazed, ashen looks. They were emerging from cover, discovering what had happened to their Monticello.

A widespread power outage froze electric clocks at 5:17 p.m. I grasped the chilling reality that the storm had hit fewer than 15 minutes before I arrived.

Ernie's directive had placed me moments away from the midst of one of the most destructive tornadoes in the 20th century.

Instead, I was about to chronicle its aftermath.

***

I captured all that I could in my notebook as I made my way to the center of the city.

Each block seemed more devastated than the last. Weaving through rubble, I was dumbstruck to find the 10-block business area looking like a war zone.

The county courthouse, a tall limestone and steel structure that dominated the square for 80 years, was crushed. A direct hit ruined in one horrifying blow an architectural gem and symbol of rock-hard strength. Its clock tower had toppled; its roof destroyed.

<u>Courtesy Monticello Herald Journal</u>

White County Courthouse before the tornado.

After the storm, a roof toppled

My training taught me to keep focused. "Get the Who, What, When, Where, Why, and How," I thought. Surely dozens were killed and hundreds hurt.

I needed a voice of authority and found it in a makeshift state police command center. There were many injured. Worst cases were rushed to a local hospital that thankfully hadn't been obliterated.

After hours gathering facts and quotes, I realized I must call Ernie by deadline. But this was long before cell phones. Lines were down for miles.

Racing to the Chevelle, I drove for a good half-hour before I spotted lights in a rural residence. Figuring there would be a working phone, I pleaded my way to its use and called in my notes.

***

I spent much of the next week in Monticello, filing news stories and using a tiny Instamatic camera to take the first front-page photo of my newspaper career.

My reporting focused on Monticello's portion of a much larger disaster. The storms eventually were characterized as a Super Tornado outbreak.

In Monticello, roughly 350 were injured and more than $100 million sustained in damages (1974 dollars). The community had been struck by a tornado classified F4 (winds reaching 200 mph), according to the National Weather Service. The big picture was 148 tornadoes affecting 13 states in an 18-hour period, the largest number of tornadoes recorded in a single event.

The Super Tornado outbreak caused 159 deaths (34 in Xenia, Ohio) and more than 6,000 injuries. Thirty of the

148 tornadoes rated the highest classifications, F4 or F5.

Somehow, there were only eight deaths in Monticello, despite being struck by a tornado that lay waste to an area of more than half-a-mile wide. The path covered an incredible 121 miles in all, from Illinois to Rainsville to Monticello and beyond, although expert Ted Fujita later determined there were actually two tornadoes on the same path. One dissipated but was quickly replaced by another.

Forty-four years later, numerous memories remain for me. One came from touring damage with a local official. Amid rubble on the courthouse lawn, I spotted a heavy block cornerstone. Noting its date, I assumed it was from the courthouse.

Not so. The official recognized the cornerstone from another smashed building, a few blocks away.

***

Two days after the storm, April 5, was the day I met Karen Stotts.

Once again, Ernie Wilkinson triggered the story. "Denny, you need to interview the girl who survived in the river. Get over to St. Elizabeth Hospital."

St. Elizabeth was not far from my office, in next-door Lafayette. Seventeen-year-old Karen was taken there to treat a concussion.

State Police had told me about Karen's incredible— and heartbreaking—story in time for my coverage in that morning's newspaper. Initial facts were sketchy and inaccurate (including misspelling her name. That happens in chaos accompanying a breaking story).

But the most tragic elements were accurate: Karen was a passenger in a van passing through Monticello, crossing a bridge over the Tippecanoe River. The

VAN BUS PULLED FROM RIVER
5 Feared Drowned in Vehicle

tornado snatched the van from the bridge and tossed it into water more than 50 feet below.

Others in the van were killed, the driver and four other teenage girls. But Karen, seated in the rear, swam out of the vehicle. Despite the fall and swift current, she struggled to safety. A woman near the river bank answered her cries for help.

Courtesy Indianapolis Star

The day after the tornado struck, April 4, was when I used my inexpensive Instamatic to photograph the van as it was recovered by a large crane. I later learned that one of the young girls' bodies was still inside.

By the next morning, April 5, Ernie knew Karen had been taken to St. Elizabeth. I would interview her there.

***

"I think it's a miracle that I'm alive," she told me, and that quote became the lead of my page one article on April 6. It was my first front-page story as a full-time news reporter.

Karen was propped up in her hospital bed. She looked small and delicate, and she was calm. Surprisingly so, I thought.

As we spoke, divers searched for all of her fellow passengers except the young woman whose body was in the van pulled from the river.

Donald Richards, their seminary teacher, had been driving Karen and the other teens back to Fort Wayne, where she was a senior at North High School. The group was returning from an educational tour at Nauvoo, Illinois.

"The weather was calm, but black outside," she said. "We turned right onto the bridge and the wind started blowing. At first, I thought it was hail that started hitting us (the van). But it must have been sticks and stones."

At that point, Richards told his students to get on the floor. But wind rolled the vehicle over and over and off the bridge.

She remembered hitting the water, nose down, the rear window exploding, feeling someone else under the water, and then "we were swept away in different directions."

The van landed about 10 feet from concrete bridge supports, but Karen couldn't reach them as she thrashed to stay afloat.

She reached a point "when I felt I was going to die and was ready to die, but something clicked in my mind and I knew I wouldn't." Rolling on her back helped. Karen saw houses and tried to make it toward them. Finally, her head bumped a branch. She grabbed it and pulled herself to shore.

Reviewing my yellowed news clipping from 1974, I wondered if our roles were reversed, would I have been as composed as the brown-haired teen—just two days after it happened.

I closed my '74 article as it had begun—by letting Karen speak.

"I love each and every one of them very much," she said. "They are with the Lord. When He calls people, that's the way it is. He just didn't want me to go now.

"Someday, I'll be with them again."

***

Retirement brings the gift of time. This ended my decades-long excuse for not contacting Karen.

In June 2017, I Googled "Karen Stotts and tornado." There I found *"In the Path of the Tornado,"* an article written by Karen Stotts Myatt. It had been published in

2008 by *Ensign*, a magazine for The Church of Jesus Christ of Latter-Day Saints (LDS).

We connected on Facebook and spoke by phone several days before she turned 61. She called from her car, stronger of voice but with the same calm, straightforward manner.

After 43 years, we had another interview.

I learned that the young woman who converted to the LDS faith just eight months before her fateful trip went on to do missionary work, also serving as an LDS educator for more than 20 years. Karen teaches courses including college level. Donald Richards would no doubt be proud.

Karen lives in Sandy, Utah, about 20 miles south of Salt Lake City. She married Ronald Myatt a little more than five years after Monticello. When we spoke, their "three beautiful kids" were 35, 33, and 31.

Are you OK, Karen?

"I have my moments," she said. "I still have some PTSD—getting worse, actually. I suspect that's because of my age. But I've never put this subject in the 'don't want to talk about it' category.

"It was difficult to stay in Fort Wayne," she said. "All the families (of victims) cried when they saw me." So she moved first to Salt Lake, then California, then back to Utah. But she keeps in touch with two of the families.

Karen recalls initially being taken to the hospital in Monticello. There, where so many people had cuts and broken bones, she was released because she had no readily apparent serious injuries. But the next morning, good Samaritans she stayed with noticed Karen forking a countertop instead of her scrambled eggs. That's how she wound up at St. Elizabeth, treated for a concussion.

Turns out she also pulled back muscles, an injury that still bothers her. "But I've led a productive life. I decided long ago you don't get over anything like this. It's always going to be with me. God helps you get through it."

She's never returned to Monticello, though she was invited. It didn't work out timewise. She returned to Illinois with her family for the 2002 dedication of the new Nauvoo Temple, which has great significance for the LDS church and its members.

The original temple was destroyed in the 1800s, mostly by fire and the rest, ironically, by a tornado. The church bought land in Nauvoo in 1937, determined to continue its presence in the land where Joseph Smith and Brigham Young played key roles in the origins of Mormonism. Karen wrote in the magazine that she carried an unnecessary burden of guilt for many years. "I was spared from death while four talented and lovely young women and our seminary teacher were not." Eventually, her feelings changed. "I knew I had been meant to remain on earth to finish my course." I asked whether I had caused her further pain with our interview on April 5, 1974.

No. In fact, it took a while for Karen to remember me.

As someone who lived through unspeakable tragedy, she had this advice for professionals like me:

"Sensitivity," she urged. "I cringe when I see how victims are interviewed on TV...questions get asked that reach the point of being crass."

That's not me, Karen, or at least not the journalist I've tried to be. I wish you the best, and I so appreciate the opportunity to speak with you. Again.

Writing Tip #7—Plan Before You Write

It's tempting to sit at the keyboard and pound away without forming a plan, but don't do it.

This wisdom from Writing Coach Don Fry has stuck with me for decades: "Five minutes of organization saves me five hours of headaches." Sounds like a gross exaggeration. It's not.

You wouldn't take a trip without GPS or a hand-held map. Similarly, you need to map out where you're headed when you're writing an article, a short story, or longer. The outlining process can help you spot trouble, such as where you need to do further research on a topic. It can also build confidence: "Hey, I've got really good material, and here's a sound, logical way to proceed."

When I was a rookie in the newsroom, I fell into the trap of "frantic flipping" through my notebook. Frantic flippers try to build an article in their mind, and then find facts they've gathered one at a time to build the story. Not good!

Fortunately, I had access to colleagues and writing coaches who suggested better ways. One that I adopted was to first make a brief outline of what had to be in my story. I would label these key topics A through D, no more than E. I would then go through my notebook with a colored pen or pencil, circling notes that fell into those groups, marking them with the appropriate letter, A to D.

During this phase, I also look for what in those groupings jumped out as a possible beginning or ending (also called a "kicker") for the article. And I would determine the best order for my material: hypothetically, ordering the story with "C" followed by "A," then "B" and so on.

Now that the plan is locked in, it's time to start writing. Follow the blueprint. This method of organizing served me well for decades.

The Power of the Press

Herbert Howe was an associate professor of geosciences at Purdue University in the 1970s. Google him today, and you'll find that Howe authored such journal articles as *"Carbonate Rocks of Montoya Group of Trans-Pecos, Texas."* Valuable to someone, certainly, but not everyday reading material for most of us.

Howe also was a paleontologist. Paleontologists study fossils, including past life forms.

It was the paleontology connection that brought us together in November 1975. Within days of our meeting, Herbert Howe would become something of a celebrity, an authority quoted across the United States. An authority on the Loch Ness monster.

And all because I had a slow news day.

I was northern Indiana reporter in a one-person news bureau, and it was dead quiet in late November. I had no leads, no tips, nothing on my events calendar.

This wasn't good, with Editor Ernie calling.

He wanted to know what I'd contribute to upcoming issues of *The Indianapolis Star*, which begged for copy during the usually slow Thanksgiving week.

Desperation set in. Flipping through pages of recent news for inspiration, I unearthed a nugget.

Those old enough will recall the story that grabbed my attention. A researcher had taken photographs at a deep lake in Scotland called Loch Ness. His images claimed to show a legendary elusive creature: the Loch Ness monster.

The newspaper account said the researcher's photos depict "flippers of the same general shape in the fossil records of prehistoric reptiles."

Bingo.

I knew that among its ocean of experts, nearby Purdue had a geosciences department. Was this salvation for my news-starved moment? Could I be lucky enough to provide a local angle, quoting someone about this raging international speculation?

I phoned a university contact. Luckily, he remembered a prof who considered this very topic "something of a hobby."

Prof. Howe graciously accepted an interview. Not only was he willing to discuss "Nessie," he had his own theory: If the monster is somehow real, it could be a plesiosaur. Or, an ichthyosaur.

A what? Or a what?

The two types of dinosaurs Howe identified lived in the Jurassic Period of the Mesozoic Era, many millions of years ago. Finding one of these alive in modern times may sound preposterous, he admitted. But Howe said that since fossils of sharks date to before the time of the dinosaurs, it could be possible for a dinosaur to exist in Loch Ness. After all, sharks thrive, millions of years later.

***

Along about now, you'd think this conversation was something out of *Jurassic Park*. But Spielberg's movie wouldn't come along for 18 years after our interview.

Howe pulled out reference materials to show me that the plesiosaur was the approximate length of what supposedly had been seen in Scotland, particularly due to its long neck. But he said the ichthyosaur was even more probable at Loch Ness because of its fish-like characteristics. Those would be necessary to survive in the water.

***

Today, Herbert Howe is retired. Skepticism has turned to total disbelief for most people whenever the Loch Ness monster is mentioned. But at the time, coverage of the supposed find made front-page news.

So it wasn't odd when my article quoting Howe in 1975 was allowed more than 20 inches of space across a section front. The story was accompanied by drawings of the plesiosaur and ichthyosaur, generated by our staff artist.

Editor Ernie was happy. I was, too, and relieved. I'd come through when the paper needed me. I went back to chasing new assignments and enjoying Thanksgiving weekend.

A couple of weeks passed. I hadn't heard from the professor, so I called to make sure he was OK with how I'd featured him in a statewide newspaper.

No problem with the article, Howe said. But he confessed to being overwhelmed. That's because he'd been on the phone about the story for days, besieged by reporters and broadcasters from as far away as Boston and Houston and England, even.

Turned out portions of my article had been picked up broadly by *The Associated Press*, circulated in newspapers, and quoted on television. Howe and his theory about the Loch Ness monster had become the subject of school class projects in other states. When not on the phone, he was answering letters from people inquiring about the monster, prehistoric creatures, and so forth.

"It's really amazing how this thing has snowballed," he said.

My encounter with Howe blessedly occurred before the full-blown rise of cable news and social media. Otherwise, I surely would have seen him on CNN or web pages including those for *Science* and *Prehistoric Times* magazines.

Even today, nearly 45 years later, I was able to find evidence of Howe's comments quoted in such far-flung archives as those of the *Beatrice (Nebraska) Daily Sun* ("If You Didn't See It in the Sun, It Didn't Happen") and the *Fergus Falls (Minnesota) Daily Journal*. The *AP's* reach is far and wide.

Decades ago, in my follow-up call to the professor to see how things were going, he was disappointed to learn the researcher's "photographs of Nessie" were found to be suspicious. But Howe still believed it technically possible for a prehistoric species to survive. He told me about the coelacanth, a fish species discovered in the depths of the Indian Ocean. That fish was thought to have been disappeared at least 50 million years ago.

***

The Herbert Howe episode was an important lesson for a young news reporter. The news won't always come to you. So be creative, anticipate the quiet times and plan for them.

As years passed in my journalism career, I had many other stories "with legs" like this one, circulating widely, a few even in *The New York Times*.

Thanks to Herbert Howe, my slow news days were becoming extinct.

Writing Tip #8—Beginnings and Endings

It's always key to grab the reader's attention at the start and finish with a flourish.

If you're writing a news article, the intro to the story (or lede, as journalists know it) is critical. You want to convince the audience to read on, as I tried to achieve with this opening paragraph in a story about a huge ranch in northwest Indiana:

"Merlin Karlock is an Illinois man with an Indiana ranch that looks like it belongs deep in the heart of Texas."

If the headline and first paragraph of a news story don't grab you, the rest of the story could be tossed aside. So keen attention to beginnings is essential, similar to how the first chapter in a book will set expectations for what follows.

Is a lede a summary, as I wrote in the story about Merlin Karlock? Not necessarily. So-called "suitcase ledes" that are overloaded with too much information can be bland.

So how about beginning with a great quote? Again, this is not necessarily a good idea. It's up to the writer to craft what the story is about and pull readers in through an inviting, surprising, or intriguing approach. Your lede can extend to two or even three paragraphs.

I used to craft beginnings in my mind after I had finished reporting. That often worked for me. But when the lede didn't come quickly to me, I frequently would obsess so much about it that it slowed my progress on

105

writing the article. I've learned that it's better to simply dive into the piece to be written and then go back and write the beginning later. Often your lede becomes obvious once you're into the story.

As to endings: I've learned to appreciate good ones that take the reader back to the top of the article, as if tying up a package with a bow. It's important to avoid trailing off at the end. Find an interesting nugget of information or a special quote to end a piece while organizing your story. This technique will save time while helping you finish with a flourish.

Final observation: if it comes down to having a better beginning than an ending, the choice is obvious. Grab attention at the start, and then challenge yourself to pull readers to the end.

She Reached for the Sky

We all have regrets. One of mine is not reconnecting with Janice Voss.

Oh, what stories she could share from her too-short life.

I met Janice in December of 1975 when she was 19, full of promise and enthusiasm. I was researching a story about the growing number of women studying engineering, a traditionally male domain.

I'd lined up an interview with Christy Smith, coordinator for women in engineering at Purdue University.

Many thanks to Christy for bringing Janice along. Because Janice became the heart of my story.

At the time, Janice was near graduation, serving as a teaching assistant. She was completing a five-year program in engineering science at one of the nation's toughest engineering schools in three and a half years—with a perfect grade average.

Very impressive, but there's more. Janice Voss accomplished this while working toward her goal of becoming an astronaut. This at a time when no U.S. women had been to space, a fact that had my pen scribbling furiously in my notebook.

Fifteen years later, Janice achieved her goal. She became part of the crews on five Space Shuttle missions. She wound up spending more than 49 days in space and traveling nearly 19 million miles.

***

107

Janice blasted off for space for the first time in 1993. But according to John Norberg, author of *"Wings of Our Dreams: Purdue in Flight,"* she almost didn't get to live her dream.

She first applied for the astronaut program in 1978. "But Janice wasn't accepted, and didn't get accepted until her fourth try," John told me. "Even then, her friends had to talk her into it (applying again). She didn't know if she could accept another failure."

During her time at Purdue, Janice participated in a co-op program that took her to Johnson Space Center at Houston to work with computer simulations of space shuttle programs. She attended graduate school at Massachusetts Institute of Technology after Purdue, armed with the Lillian M. Gilbreth Scholarship. Janice was selected for that scholarship out of 128 applicants representing 67 schools.

Even with these credentials and more work she'd done for NASA, she had been rejected three times to be an astronaut.

But then she got her chance. And she did our nation proud.

***

In my 1975 article, Janice said this: "I have been encouraged by my complete acceptance at Purdue and the Space Center in an area which has been considered 'male' for so many years."

At the time of that interview, only 20,000 of the 1.5 million engineers in the U.S. were women. The number grew to more than 190,000 of them by 2004. It's greater still today.

Why no female astronauts by 1975? "The original astronauts were all military people," Janice told me. "They were trained to operate the spacecraft. But with the space shuttle, lots of scientists will be taken along as passengers. They won't be subjected to physical hardship."

Once NASA selected Janice for the astronaut program (1990), she became the first woman among what is now a group of 25 astronauts with Purdue ties. She began a nearly 20-year astronaut career that featured two flights aboard shuttle Endeavour (1993 and 2000).

In between the Endeavour expeditions, Janice flew on Discovery in 1995. It was the first time for the shuttle to rendezvous with a Russian space station, Mir. She maneuvered a robot arm to grasp an astronomy satellite on that flight.

Her next space journey, aboard Columbia, was shortened when fuel cells malfunctioned. The same crew lifted off again several months later with Janice aboard as payload commander, responsible for experiments that included setting more than 140 small fires in insulation chambers. The goal was testing the behavior of fire in weightlessness, monitoring safety concerns that stemmed from a 90-second fire onboard Mir months earlier.

Janice also coordinated experiments with plants, more than 50 of them including spinach, clover, sage, and periwinkle.

After her last flight in 2000, Janice continued with NASA. One job was serving as science director for the upcoming mission of the Kepler spacecraft/telescope, which went on to discover more than 2,600 planets outside our solar system.

I would loved to have talked to Janice about any of this. I wondered, for example, if in leading the fire experiments on Columbia, her thoughts ever turned to Gus Grissom (B.S., mechanical engineering, '50) and Roger Chaffee (B.S., aeronautical engineering, '57), who died in a flash fire while training for what would have been their flight on Apollo 1.

I wondered how it felt to achieve a goal that had to seem so far away in childhood. What was it like to be one of only six women who have flown in space five times, or to see Earth while orbiting so far above, and other questions that I could never ask for this book because…

***

…Cancer took Janice from us in 2012. She was only 55 years old.

Janice had been diagnosed with breast cancer at 45, Norberg said. By all accounts, she confronted the perils of her cancer journey with an upbeat attitude and a fierce determination to keep working and contributing.

Her legacy at NASA is profound, according to Peggy Whitson, who spent 665 days in space herself and performed four spacewalks (so much for women not enduring physical hardship). Whitson was chief of the astronaut corps when Janice died.

"Janice was responsible for paving the way for experiments that we now perform on a daily basis on the International Space Station," Whitson said in a press statement.

Norberg, retired reporter for the Lafayette *Journal & Courier,* has become a leading authority on Purdue astronauts and is an author of other Purdue-related books.

"I interviewed Janice a number of times," he said. "She frequently came back to campus over the years and was very supportive of Purdue and women in engineering."

Purdue students helped to return the favor. In 2015, dedication ceremonies were held for VOSS (Visiting Our Solar System), a $1.5 million outdoor exhibit of the solar system named for Janice that includes a

version of the sun that is 45 feet in diameter, surrounded by scale models of each of the planets. The monument to Janice and her remarkable life is open to the public and tour groups, "and is really, really special," John said.

"I've learned there are two different types of astronauts. Janice was very different from many of them, who have their noses stuck to the window in their spare time. Janice was no window-gazer. She was fascinated by the technology.

"She spent a lot of her time writing to family and friends, wanting to share her experience with them while she was experiencing it, sharing the technical, scientific aspects."

Janice's parents, Louise and Jim, both Purdue graduates, remembered how their daughter became fascinated with space travel at 9 years old when she read "*A Wrinkle in Time*" by Madeleine L'Engel.

Decades later, John said, "she re-read the book on one of her flights."

To honor their daughter, Louise and Jim established the Janice E. Voss Scholarship for Women in Engineering at Purdue, where women have gone from less than 1 percent of the engineering enrollment to 20 percent of the undergraduate engineering degrees.

You were the trailblazer, Janice. Good for you.

Writing Tip #9—The Peril of Unanswered Questions

Readers will be distracted or lose interest if you leave loose ends dangling.

Ginger and I were watching a sad report on TV news. Police video was available for the first time of an incident involving a man who shot three police officers on what initially seemed a routine call. A veteran cop died of his wounds.

The video was the reason for the story on TV news. Left unsaid, however, was what had happened to the shooter. Was he charged, tried, convicted? The report didn't say. Evidently, the station believed that previous stories covered that fact, so it was no longer necessary to repeat it.

Wrong! I raise this as an example of an unanswered question. In this case, the station ignored viewers who were new to this story.

Unanswered questions are stumble points for readers and viewers, distracting from the seamless order of content that characterizes the best storytelling.

If a short story or book introduces us to several characters or threads of storylines and abandons some of them, why introduce them in the first place?

(There is an exception, of course. Fiction writers have much more latitude in story construction and dealing with characters and story threads. A whodunit writer, for example, may introduce many characters to keep readers guessing.)

But in nonfiction, especially newswriting, unanswered questions are problematic. Another "stopper" for readers is the failure to build good transitions.

I have three recommendations for avoiding these stop signs:

The first is that "every story stands on its own." In the TV example, one sentence about the status of the accused is all that would have been needed. This respects the audience that is new to a continuing story.

My second recommendation takes us back to a journalistic maxim. As you review your work, do a mental tally to ensure you have covered the "Who, What, Where, Why, and How." It's a reliable checklist.

Third, there is no shame in admitting facts that are unknown in a text. This anticipates a reader's question and lets the reader know we're anticipating your question. As an example, in a report of a celebrity death: "Authorities said the cause of death has yet to be determined." Satisfied, the reader continues to read on without getting stuck on an unanswered question.

Showdown

We all encounter situations when grave consequences ride on the outcome.

One came for me in my third year as city editor of Indiana's largest newspaper.

In 1985, I argued a critical issue with someone who had been an executive of *The Indianapolis Star* longer than I'd been alive.

Fail, and I would lose the respect of my staff, my faith in quality journalism, and, likely even the physical well-being of many readers.

***

I was appointed city editor in 1982, to the surprise of myself and Ginger. We'd been married one year.

City Editor was a very big deal back then, leading a staff of more than 50 reporters and editors. Virtually everyone in the newsgathering operation outside of the women's (later renamed Life/Style) and sports departments reported to me.

Two respected leaders held the position before I did—Larry"Bo" Connor, for 16 years, and his replacement, Dick Cady. There was quite a buzz when Cady stepped down after three years, with speculation about who'd be next.

I was pretty new to headquarters at *The Star*. My first six years as a full-time reporter were spent in the Purdue-Lafayette Bureau, 63 miles away. I was still acquainting with many of my main office colleagues, having served briefly as assistant city editor and then state editor since being promoted from Lafayette. Reporters knew that I was conscientious with their copy, but still considered me a new guy given my work at the bureau.

Connor had been elevated to managing editor, so this was his decision. When he summoned me in May of '82, I hadn't applied and expected him to ask who I thought would be best for the job. It never occurred to me I'd be his choice. Others had more experience and, heck, I was 33 years old.

In offering the job to me Connor chose someone who had never led more than three direct reports, unless you count time in college at the *Indiana Daily Student* or as a squad leader in Basic Training.

Wowsers.

***

Bo gave me the following Memorial Day weekend to think it over. So much for our relaxing first anniversary celebration at the French Lick Springs Hotel.

How could you not take the job? It meant more pay, opportunity, and deeper immersion in the profession I loved. That's immersion as in ocean, rather than puddle.

Talk about responsibility. Not only would more than 50 people see me as their boss, but I'd have considerable say about what news would be consumed by subscribers, then more than 200,000 daily and 400,000 on Sunday. I would also be in for a sacrifice of personal life that can't be recovered.

After much back and forth that overwhelmed anniversary celebrating, Ginger and I decided I'd take the job.

Weeks later at a party, Cady's wife confided to Ginger that Dick had "done you no favors." Bo himself acknowledged the demanding/rewarding pull and tug of the city editor's job in his book, *"Star in the Hoosier Sky."*

***

Here's what my first day was like: the city room was under renovation, so desks were shielded with plastic from dust clouds raised by hammers and saws.

We were wrestling with a new phone system.

And Business Editor Mike McNamee swung by sheepishly to inform me that he was taking a job with a new venture known as *USA Today*: "Sorry about the timing," he said.

That was the beginning. Over the years we were awakened many times with calls from apologetic night editors seeking input on late-breaking news. Another call caused me to throw my clothes back on and drive across town to visit an older reporter making worrisome comments about his life.

My family and I were threatened by a mentally unstable man.

I hired and fired, consoled, and, I hope, inspired. I was taken advantage of by slackers and wowed by colleagues who couldn't do enough for me and the profession they loved.

I gave speeches and represented the paper at many events. In the "everything rolls downhill" category, Bo delegated the crowning of a fair queen. The published picture shows me looking skyward as I did the honors, not wanting to be photographed eyeing the contents of a low-cut dress.

I defended myself against those who wondered why we "didn't do things the way we'd done them for years," collapsing in a hallway one awfully stressful day. A reporter helped me up and it was back to fighting deadlines.

I fielded angry calls about our coverage, had limited success in creating a more diverse newsroom, and survived a libel lawsuit.

I also took a phone call in 1991 awarding the Pulitzer Prize for our team's work on medical malpractice in Indiana. *The Star* hasn't won another since (as of 2021).

***

Bo Connor gave me plenty of rope as city editor, probably because he had worked for a managing editor who was an overbearing, hands-on tyrant.

I tried to emulate Bo as a manager. Let good reporters and editors have the kind of freedom I appreciated and they will make you proud. Provide advice when they need it and otherwise keep in touch at arms' length. Edit in a way that doesn't stifle creativity but insists on accurate, fair articles that are clear and respectful of the reader.

Gosh knows, we weren't perfect and winced when we were scooped. But we excelled on our good days. At least two judges were imprisoned or removed from the bench following our brave reporting. I was never prouder than when our staff-owned coverage of the Pan Am Games in 1987, a huge event for Indianapolis.

Another one of our greatest achievements was preceded by crisis. That's the one that began this story.

***

I had never been to Bill Dyer's office. I knew the man well enough to say hello.

In October 1985, Bill sent my world reeling. Just a few words from him made me upset, angry, disillusioned, knotted in the stomach, and terrified—yes, terrified—of how I would convey Bill's shocking directive to *The Star* staff.

William A. Dyer Jr., born in 1902, was still on the job at the age of 83 as president of Indianapolis Newspapers Inc., publisher of *The Star*. Bill ran the business side, something he'd been involved with since he was hired in 1944.

Bill wasn't just a towering figure status-wise; he was a very big man. His office was a throne-like setting, with a massive desk and his massive presence seated behind. The place reeked of authority.

Bill met with me to discuss something that had been progressing in our newsroom for half a year.

***

Special project work is vital for newspapers (and other respected media channels). It's also a privilege for reporters who earn the chance to do it.

Special projects are necessary because you can't dig deeply into truly important stories in just a day or even a week. The work is a privilege because those assigned have the freedom to work for months or longer while the rest of the staff pounds out daily and Sunday coverage.

Watergate began as a small-time break-in at a political office, but Woodward and Bernstein pursued that skulduggery for two years. *The Star's* 1991 Pulitzer required a year from the first research until publication.

Early in 1985, two of our top reporters pitched a project of vast importance. Vic Caleca and Richard D. "Dick" Walton, veterans of the science and medicine beats, wanted to write about cancer. And they wanted to do it in a comprehensive way that would cover the terrible toll cancers take on lives in Indiana and beyond. They wanted to explore available treatments and research and convey the personal impact on patients, caregivers, and families. They knew that *The Star* had covered this story piecemeal and emphasized that it was time to give it the priority of time and commitment it deserved.

Should we? No-brainer. Project Editor Linda Caleca (who came to us from Chicago, where she led wire service coverage) would oversee the team's work, with regular input to me. Chief Photographer Jerry Clark, another top talent, would work alongside the reporters.

We informed Connor and moved forward with his blessing. I was excited we would expose facts not widely known to our audience and potentially even save lives. As part of the coverage, we'd give readers the best known ways to avoid and fight this deadly disease.

I was confident this series of articles not only would deliver **A+** work, but expeditiously: Vic and Dick craved regular bylines and wouldn't want to be away from them long. And Linda is a getting-things-done whirlwind.

The series was in the works 10 years before a controversial *60 Minutes* interview with former tobacco executive Jeff Wigand, who disclosed some of the industry's secrets about the addictiveness of cigarette smoking. This work by Walton and the Calecas would be cutting-edge.

***

I was touched by a couple of personal angles gathered by Dick and Vic as they conducted more than 150 interviews across the state and nation.

One was their interview with cancer patient Don Schlundt. Schlundt's name was of special interest to me since he was one of the greatest basketball players ever at my alma mater, Indiana University. I never got to meet Don, but as sports editor of the student newspaper, I was well aware of his accomplishments.

Vic and Dick also interviewed John Seffrin, chairman of the Indiana division of the American Cancer Society. I knew John from the 1970s when I played pickup basketball with him at Purdue, where he was a health educator.

The Walton/Caleca team worked diligently for five months. That's what it takes to pull together an eight-part series and the editing process. Publication was set for early November 1985.

But Bill Dyer had learned of our plans.

***

Ordinarily, Dyer had minimal involvement in *The Star's* editorial content. Publisher Eugene S. Pulliam was ultimately in charge but relied on Bo Connor's leadership. Bo and I met regularly about plans for the daily and Sunday editions.

Gene and Bo were aware of the series' progress. Bo, a terrific newsman, was as excited as we all were about it.

A series would, however, require extra hundreds of inches of newsprint. On those occasions, it was up to Gene to "bump up" the size of the paper to accommodate the need.

As leader of business operations, Dyer would be informed that the newspaper must reconfigure with added news space.

Unbeknownst to me, he balked.

Not because of space needed for the cancer series. No, he had another reason.

***

Bo called me to his office. "Denny," he said somberly, "Dyer doesn't want the series to run."

I'd known Bo since 1970. Nothing he'd ever said hit harder. At first, I thought he was joking. It was unthinkable to throw away an important series and nearly half a year's work by top people.

"We can postpone a week if we have to," I said. "What's up?"

Connor, who had read and praised the first several articles, said additional space wasn't the issue. "Bill thinks we'll demoralize readers. The stories are so powerful and frank about pain and suffering that he thinks they're too upsetting."

Upsetting? In a newspaper known for its coverage of murders and terrible accidents and a paper that, over the years, devoted thousands of inches to deadly tornadoes and floods?

Upsetting? What about the positive nature of warning Hoosiers about the importance of lifestyle changes to help avoid cancer or detect it early?

Upsetting? When the role of a newspaper is to inform its readers, not shield them?

Particularly stunning was how Eugene S. Pulliam, the publisher/owner, a thoughtful man who understood—and paid for—good journalism, could be overruled by Dyer.

"This can't happen, Bo," I pleaded. "We've got to change his mind."

***

Bill Dyer was hired in the 1940s when Eugene C. Pulliam, Eugene S. Pulliam's father, was publisher/owner of *The Star*. The elder Pulliam did many good things for Indianapolis but also didn't hesitate to control the newspaper's content.

As a result, *The Star* earned its stridently conservative reputation under his management. Gene C. ordered positive coverage of his favored candidates for Congress and the White House. He was so opposed to Bobby Kennedy's candidacy in 1968 that news of Kennedy's famous speech in Indianapolis on the day Martin Luther King was assassinated was relegated to an inside page. Other newspapers carried the same story prominently (and appropriately, as a news event involving a respected leader).

Eugene S. Pulliam, or Gene as he insisted on being called by his employees, was different. When he moved into the publisher's office after his father's death, Gene was sympathetic to conservative causes but routinely kept those opinions on the editorial page. I recall him influencing coverage with me only once. He asked that a reference to a candidate he favored be moved higher in an article than the "jump," or the continued portion of the story inside the paper. I didn't think it was worth debating, so I complied.

Pulliam did defer to Dyer, however. As I've mentioned, Dyer was older than Gene and a holdover from Eugene C. Pulliam's front office.

Young Gene was willing to do this much: when Bo told him I'd asked to appeal Dyer's decision, he arranged a meeting in Bill's office on an upper floor of *The Star's* then-headquarters at 307 North Pennsylvania Street.

***

Five of us went to Dyer's office: me, Gene, Bo, and reporters Walton and Caleca.

We were greeted warmly. I was directed to a chair in front of the massive desk, with the others around and behind me. This vibe made it clear that Gene and Bo already had been heard on this subject; ours was a courtesy appeal. Not encouraging.

Still, I made an impassioned plea. I was near tears as I looked in Dyer's face, wound up with emotion and determination. But this was no time to show weakness.

I emphasized the importance of this series to Indianapolis and Indiana, given the gravity of the subject matter. I detailed the extensive effort by outstanding reporters and the potentially life-saving effect we would have on at least some of our readers.

All were met with a polite reaction.

"It's just too painful," Dyer said. "I know the stories are well-researched and written, that's not the point. We go into people's homes at breakfast. We have to consider the negative impact. I'm sorry. My mind's made up."

He also told us that he feared *The Star* would lose circulation when readers disapproved, conceding "we don't know what the reaction might be."

An exasperated Walton couldn't hold his tongue. "When you do know," he said caustically, "get back to us."

You can only imagine how the reporters felt at that moment—given mountains of work, time spent with ailing cancer victims and their families who wanted to tell their stories, and months of encouragement from the newsroom chain of command.

Devastated, they left the room. I asked to remain, as did Gene and Bo.

I simply couldn't give in. Mustering my most sincere expression, I said there would almost certainly be consequences. "These are loyal reporters who could get hired anywhere else," I said. "They've done everything we asked and then some. I hate to say it, but they will likely leave the newspaper over this and others might, too. It would be hard to blame them, Bill."

Dyer remained unmoved. "You are representing your staff well," he said. "But I've made my decision. I do thank you for coming."

Bo patted me on the shoulder. It was time to go. Gene lingered as Bo and I headed downstairs.

***

It's odd what you remember about episodes like this. I can still feel myself slumping into a chair at Bo's office, anguished and defeated. He shut the door behind me, something he rarely did. "I'm sorry," Bo said.

And then he shared the real reason for Bill's decision.

Dyer's wife had been treated for cancer. He was being protective, not wanting her to read a week's worth of extensive coverage about a subject plaguing their lives.

I shook my head. "We can't let that influence an entire readership," I mumbled.

My thoughts turned to having to face staffers with this disheartening news. So much work down the drain, such a slap at our journalistic mission, and why? There was no way to tell them, but it had to be done.

Then, a knock on the door.

***

In came Gene.

"Denny," he said. "You did it. Bill says you're quite a salesman.

"He said go ahead and publish. After the first day, he wants the rest of the stories to play lower on Page One. He said go ahead and win awards."

R-E-L-I-E-F. Thank heavens. Thanks Bill, thanks to the alignment of the moon and stars, thanks to whoever or whatever.

It would be easy for me to take the credit, to consider myself a hero. I didn't and I wasn't. This was the right thing to do.

I also would like to think, and maybe should think, that Gene weighed in one last time with Dyer and won the day. He and I never spoke about this again. We didn't need to.

We had a series to publish.

***

The series dominated state contests with first-place awards. It prompted numerous letters to the editor, the majority praising how eye-opening, well written, informative and beneficial the series had been.

One comment special to me didn't make it into print. For 10 weeks in the fall of 1985, I was a juror in a civil case. That meant I did my jury duty by day, racing to the newspaper for several hours of evening city editor work.

127

One fellow juror was a physician. During the trial, we had discussed how proud I was of the series (pre-publication). After *"Cancer: The Longest War"* made it into print, she gushed how impressed she had been with the articles.

By the time the series appeared, Don Schlundt had died at 52. He passed away two months after being interviewed, when Dick and Vic had found the 6-foot, 10-inch sports legend "gaunt and weak." I still recall with admiration how Don and his wife, Gloria, candidly discussed his experience. They shared with others, to their everlasting credit.

John Seffrin was a voice of authority in the series, explaining the prevalence of cancer and the importance of good lifestyle habits, including not smoking. My Purdue friend later became CEO of the American Cancer Society for 22 years, transforming it into the world's largest voluntary organization fighting cancer.

Vic Caleca went on to become one of my successors as city editor of *The Star*. His wife, Linda, also edited our Pulitzer-winning effort. She worked with me not only at the newspaper but later in communications at Eli Lilly and Company. These are two of the best journalists I've ever met and cherished friends.

Walton died in 2015 and Clark two years later. Walton, another good friend, was a dedicated reporter, writer, and one of the funniest people I've ever known. He wrote a humor column, *"Punch Lines,"* that I always looked forward to reading. Clark was a talented photographer and a fine person.

Early 2021 brought the shocking news that Vic Caleca died after a sudden illness. I miss his friendship and wise counsel, as do so many others who knew him.

Gene Pulliam died in 1999 and the newspaper that had been owned by his family for more than half a century was sold to the corporate giant Gannett. Bill Dyer died six years earlier, at 90. He was still working regularly before he died.

Bo Connor, one of my greatest influences, died in 2014 at the age of 88. He had retired in 1990. In *"Star in the Hoosier Sky,"* Bo wrote this: "I've forgotten how many prizes we won for the series, but I know it convinced a lot of readers to stop smoking, including me."

Writing Tip #10 — Editing, Part I

Prune excess wording and speed your sentences. Your readers will appreciate it.

I've mentioned Larry "Bo" Connor in this memoir a few times, with good reason. He was instrumental in my career at *The Indianapolis Star* in many ways, including this one.

In the mid-1970s, I worked with reporter Bruce Smith on a series about landlords who were taking advantage of college students by renting run-down housing at inflated prices.

The article we submitted was wordy, flabby, and not as crisp as it should have been.

Bo Connor was overwhelmed with work as city editor (something I later learned about that job myself). Nevertheless, he took the time to edit a printout of the story and return it to us.

What a valuable lesson this was.

I will share only one paragraph so you can see what I mean—the second paragraph of the story. We began the article with a scene-setter, a paragraph about a Purdue student who had rapped on the wall of her aged apartment, which led to plaster tumbling into her living room.

ORIGINAL VERSION:

"That's a mess, isn't it?" asks Ruth Irwin, without pausing for an answer. She beckons a visitor toward the kitchen of the apartment.

CONNOR'S EDITED VERSION:

"A mess, isn't it?" asks Ruth Irwin. She beckons toward the kitchen.

Not a meaningful word was lost. The edited version moves the story forward more quickly.

Connor did this for the entire article. I've saved his edits as a reminder for more than 45 years.

"Omit needless words" is also advice from *"The Elements of Style"* by William Strunk Jr. and E.B. White, a tiny book that reeks of wisdom. If you don't have it, get it.

Vigorous writing, according to Strunk and White, "requires not that the writer make all his sentences short, or that he avoid all detail and treat his subjects only in outline, but that every word tell."

Amen.

Yeah, It Happened to Me

Here's a selection of more accounts from my life tales. Some are sweet, some sour, some sentimental, all pried from my bank of memories.

***

My newspaper editing responsibilities included appearances at "Newspaper in Education" programs for grades 3-12 in Indianapolis and the suburbs.

Youngsters in the lower grades were the most fun.

I tried to lead off each class with a joke suitable to the age group. For the very young, I'd ask, "Where does a sheep go to get a haircut?"

(Answer: at a "baa-baa shop.")

One day I never made it to the punch line. A kid in the front row blurted:

"At a clip joint."

Topped. By an 8-year-old.

***

Good editors interact with writers when making significant changes to the reporter's copy.

Sadly, that didn't happen for me when *The Indianapolis Star* dispatched me to St. Joe, Indiana, to write a feature about a pickle factory.

Someone on the desk changed the dateline on my article from "St. Joe, Indiana" to "Saint Joseph, Indiana."

Imagine what it's like having to phone managers at Sechler's Pickles after the story appeared, reassuring them that I actually knew where I was when I spent the day with them and that I was capable of spelling the town's name.

There's an old saying that applies for editors who think they know better than the reporter on the scene:

"*Assume* makes an ass out of u and me."

***

I got word that the movie *"Hoosiers"* was going to be filmed in Indiana when I was city editor of *The Star*.

Big names (Gene Hackman, Dennis Hopper, and Barbara Hershey) were coming to act in the production about Indiana's beloved sport, basketball. It was clear to me that as the statewide newspaper, we'd have to be all over this story.

Incredibly, I couldn't get the sports department interested. This despite the fact that scenes would be filmed across the state using gymnasiums that still looked the part of the 1954 state championship won by Milan, a small school. Milan's upset ranked among the top sports stories of the 20th century in Indiana. *"Hoosiers"* was based on the story.

This story wasn't just special for Indiana; it *was* Indiana.

So I forged ahead to cover it from our news desk. I wanted a reporter to follow *"Hoosiers"* from start to finish, preferably someone who could cover filming on weekends. I selected Scott Miley, a colleague and friend.

Miley initially reacted coolly. "I'm going to chase a film crew for weeks on something the sports department passed on?" His eyes rolled.

Scott's mood changed as filming began. His reporting captured the significance of the story and the flavor of Hollywood in rural Indiana.

But here's the kicker. One Saturday, Miley appeared in the newsroom wearing a period outfit. Why? The film crew wanted to use him as a reporter posing a question to Hackman's character.

So, who's in the credits for what many (including me) consider one of the greatest sports-related films?

Yep. Scott Miley.

**

Fame may qualify a person for much popularity, but it doesn't diminish the fact that the celebrity remains as human as the rest of us.

In the 1990s I was a bureau chief based in Carmel, Indiana, with a staff responsible for covering three counties in north-suburban Indianapolis. John Flora was a member of the reporting staff.

In 1995 John teamed up with a colleague to write a touching, informative obituary for a local man named Jack Leer.

Leer was a dentist, golf course owner, and preservationist dedicated to the gray wolf species. He also was a friend of entertainer John Raitt (1917-2005), once a big Broadway star.

Raitt was coming to sing at Leer's funeral, so Flora phoned him for some comments about the deceased. In preparing for the interview, Flora noticed that pop superstar Bonnie Raitt was John's daughter. So during the interview Flora noted in passing that Bonnie's birthday was the very next day.

"It is?" Raitt gulped. "Gee, thanks for reminding me!"

***

As I mentioned in the Janice Voss chapter, covering Purdue meant opportunities to connect with astronauts who have Purdue backgrounds (as of 2020, there were 25 of them). What an opportunity for me.

In April of 1975, I spent an hour riding on a golf cart with Neil Armstrong. It hadn't been quite six years since Neil had taken a small step off a ladder to the lunar surface. Twenty-five-year-old me got to literally rub shoulders with him.

I had been cautioned not to pry about the moon flight so the modest Armstrong could spend most of his time interacting with students while he served as grand marshal of the Purdue Grand Prix go-kart race. I complied (though now I wish I hadn't).

Neil was friendly, fun, and a top-notch golf cart pilot. That day, it was his passenger who was star-struck.

***

I was driving through the Purdue campus in the late '70s when I noticed a bird fluttering helplessly along the side of the street.

Turned out it was a sickly young owl. I pulled over, put it in a cardboard box, and drove to the university's renowned veterinary school. There I was directed to Ron Winterfield, professor of avian medicine.

Even Winterfield's expertise in disease and infections in birds couldn't save the poor owl. But meeting him led to a feature story. At the time there were an estimated 25 million pet birds in the United States, and the professor's comments about their care made for good reading in *The Star*, I thought.

Winterfield had visited the Antarctic to observe penguins. I mentioned that in the story, and then realized he could help me in another way.

I was serving as program director for a local service club, the Exchange Club of Lafayette. How could I lose with this program, a slide show featuring penguins and Antarctica?

Winterfield agreed to appear. I told him ahead of time that club members (many Purdue employees) tended to leave the lunch meeting promptly at 1:30 p.m. to return to their jobs. No problem, Winterfield said. Starting at 1 p.m. would give him plenty of time.

Now, I hate to reinforce a stereotype about long-winded instructors. But Prof. Ron had a long windup and was only on his fourth or fifth slide (out of dozens) by 1:30.

By 1:45, we had only about a third of the Exchange Clubbers left in the audience even though I was frantically waving my arms, signaling Ron to speed up.

No luck. By 2 p.m., all that was left in the room was me, the professor, and a couple of my friends who were embarrassed to leave early. Winterfield was still going strong.

So maybe it is true, at least for avian experts.

Time flies.

***

In 1974 a tipster recommended that *The Star* write a feature story about a banker in northern Indiana. His name was Will Osborn, but he went by the initials "W.O."

It was somewhat surprising to meet a president and board chairman for an interview at the bank's cafeteria, not to mention a still active banker at the age of 89.

It also was surprising to learn that W.O. fed his employees free breakfast and lunch, every day, in addition to maintaining a generous wage scale.

"Pay them well, and they'll make it worth your while," said W.O., head of the State Exchange Bank of Culver and an employee there since 1906. Headquartered in a town that then had a population of just 1,700, Osborn's bank and its branches ranked in the top 8 percent of banks in the nation in a comparison of assets in relation to population.

The secret of success? Helping people.

Osborn was known for lending policies others considered too liberal. Farmers and businesses that couldn't get loans elsewhere did at the State Exchange Bank. The policies were tested during the Depression, but during that period W.O. noted that the bank never borrowed, restricted deposits, cut salaries, or skipped a dividend. In fact, the bank topped $1 million in deposits for the first time—in the Depression. Its resources were comparable to banks in much larger Bloomington and Lafayette.

Loyalty was such that people who moved out of state tended to keep their business with the State Exchange Bank because of how it had served them.

Osborn let people park their cars in the bank lot for free regardless of whether they were on bank business or shopping downtown. He allowed this because money spent downtown invariably came back to the bank. "My only regret about our lot," he told me, "is that it isn't twice as big as it already is."

As if all this weren't enough, Osborn (who died in 1981) once helped a man who robbed his bank get back on his feet, financially. He had written up some 900 wills for friends in the year prior to our interview.

My article spread the word about W.O. Years later, I spotted evidence of this on the wall of the former Morris Bryant Inn in West Lafayette, where I attended Exchange Club meetings.

Framed on the wall by a proprietor who had benefited from W.O.'s services was my article, headlined *"You Can Bank on It When You Owe 'W.O.'"*

***

I was at my desk in the Purdue-Lafayette Bureau in 1976 when I got word that a man in nearby Montgomery County wanted a reporter to come see him. The man, first name Nathan, claimed that local police had it in for his son, Roger.

I listened to the tales of alleged harassment and questionable criminal citations. Roger wasn't there for me to question, but regardless I told Nathan that, in fairness, I needed the police side of the story.

Having gathered both sides and logical explanations from the police (who, off the record, made it clear that Roger was no saint), I recommended to my editor that there was no story. I said I'd monitor the situation to see if Roger encountered more trouble in the future.

Thank heavens that was our decision.

On February 14, 1977, 24-year-old Roger Clay Drollinger and three younger men invaded a home in Parke County, Indiana, and shot-gunned four young men to death. The victims' mother survived and testified against the four men.

I never saw Nathan Drollinger again. His son and accomplices received life sentences, and Roger Drollinger died in prison in 2014.

***

My scrapbooks are filled with not only my work but from others whose writing reminds me of important moments in my life.

As I write this book in my 70th year, I notice a large number of obituaries. These are especially precious keepsakes: obits for my parents, in-laws, and for mentors, friends, and former colleagues.

Included among the obits are two people I was fortunate to know who had a significant impact on race relations.

Will Counts and Lynn Ford, more important influences on my life

Will Counts taught photography at IU and helped many outstanding photogs launch their careers. He was even patient with a so-so photographer like me.

Long before joining the faculty, Counts took one of the most powerful civil rights images ever captured while working for the *Arkansas Democrat* in Little Rock. The 1957 photo was nominated for a Pulitzer Prize. It showed 15-year-old Elizabeth Eckford, a black student, being jeered by a white student as she walked with eight other black students toward the desegregated Little Rock Central High School.

The iconic photo was captured when Counts was 26 years old. That particular day, Eckford and others in "the Arkansas nine" were blocked from entering school. They returned after President Dwight Eisenhower and federal troops intervened but still were subjected to racial slurs and frequent harassment.

Hazel Bryan (later Hazel Messery) was the white student who was pictured cruelly jeering Eckford. She later apologized to Eckford and, in 1997, reunited with her in a meeting arranged by Will Counts.

Will taught us a lot more than photography at IU. When he died at age 70, I was among many of his former students who attended the funeral service.

Lynn Ford, a black reporter I hired when I was city editor of *The Star*, also left his imprint on my life, and on many others.

Lynn started on police beat and general assignment. Recognizing Indianapolis had a sizable black community but few voices reflecting that community on our pages, we provided Lynn an occasional column that increased in frequency later in his career.

I can remember how some of his columns made me uncomfortable with his frank characterization of racial disparities in Indianapolis. Was this the same guy who, around me, most often showed an acquiescing, Teddy Bear-like personality?

Lynn and I had many in-depth conversations questioning whether he'd gone too far with his commentary. These chats were punctuated by Lynn's nodding "uh-huh, uh-huh" assents. But they were followed by columns with similar content and tone. He persevered and, in hindsight, I'm glad he did. Indianapolis was the better for it.

I had left *The Star* in early 2001 when I learned that Lynn had been stabbed. The attacker, as I recall, was a jealous boyfriend who didn't even know Lynn. I visited Lynn in Methodist Hospital, where we had a tearful reunion. I told Lynn how much I cared about him and that I was proud of him. He shared similar feelings toward me.

A year later, Lynn died of what was reported to be a heart attack. He was 43 years old.

***

Will and Lynn. Two of many who keep me revisiting the pages of my scrapbooks, fondly.

Writing Tip #11—Editing, Part II

My step-by-step editing process is one of vigorous self-editing and accepting constructive criticism.

I used a six-step editing process for each chapter in this book:

> **1. Brutal edit.** Print out the chapter. Look for the big issues: did I accomplish what I wanted to do with this piece? What did I overemphasize or under-emphasize? What's missing and what sentences or paragraphs are unnecessary or slow the piece? Does the story progression flow? By the time I've completed this first edit, my copy is very heavily marked up.

> **2. Fine-tuning.** After incorporating revisions from the brutal edit, I'm now checking accuracy in a fresh printout. I ask myself, have I confirmed the substance and timing of events in my story? Then, with a dictionary and thesaurus in hand, I check to see if in every instance I have used the most appropriate descriptions and wording. I ask, "Are my sentences front-loaded (subject followed by verb, use of active voice)." Can I prune any unnecessary words, a la Bo Connor? Am I now ready to give a printout to my wife, Ginger? (If not, revise until I am ready to do so.)

> **3. Acid test No. 1.** I print the newest version of the chapter for my wife, Ginger (find someone

you trust to do this for you). I consider her comments very seriously, as hers is the first reaction from a reader. If she doesn't understand something, I change it. You must discard your ego during this step. Here are key questions I ask Ginger: did the piece hold your interest, do you think it belongs in the book? If not, why? This is a hugely important step in the editing process. It's up to the writer to decide what to do in response to this feedback, obviously. But this step almost always produces comments that are important to the success of the piece.

4. Different perspective edit. This step may seem odd, but it works for me. I print the chapter again and take it to a different place, away from my desk. Sometimes it's another room in the house, sometimes outside on the patio, or I take it with me on a solo trip to a restaurant. The idea is to take a fresh, unhurried second look. At this point, I decide whether I'm still on the right path with the chapter or if I'm ready for....

5. Acid test No. 2. This step involves sending the piece to more people I trust who are trained writers or editors or simply wise folks I've met in my life. It helps if these are folks who have a connection to the chapter. In the case of my Chapter 10, *"Showdown,"* I am fortunate that two excellent editors, Linda and

Vic Caleca, were involved with the story and willing to help me. Not only was I able to fact-check the chapter with them, but I took advantage of their splendid editing skills.

6. Line-by-line edit. I make one more printout after incorporating the latest feedback. Now it's time to check for any typos that may have occurred in editing. By now I must feel confident that I've got a winning chapter. This is my final quality control check. Former colleague and friend John O'Neill recommended an unusual approach at this stage: read the story backwards, paragraph by paragraph, with a focus on how sentences are constructed. Are any sentences too unwieldy? Do I have good sentence variety? Are certain words repeated too often throughout the piece? This is a final, exacting step before the book reaches the publishing process.

***

What I have described is a time-consuming process. Obviously, this won't fit daily journalism. In that event, you must shrink the process to steps 1 and 2 and rely on your editors and copy editors for strong feedback.

My key message about editing is this: understand that vigorous editing is a vitally important step to revising and refining your work. If you're enjoying this book, a key reason why is the editing by myself and others that improved clunky early drafts.

Summary of Writing Tips

1. Keep a journal or diary

2. Read, read, read, because you learn much that makes you a better writer

3. Preparation is essential before you write.

4. Pursue all sides of an issue to present the best available truth.

5. Fact-check relentlessly to ensure accuracy.

6. Interviewing tips include avoid yes or no questions, listen carefully, and pose follow-ups

7. Form a plan before you write.

8. Advice on beginnings and endings

9. Avoid leaving unanswered questions in your writing that will distract readers.

10. Editing Part 1; omit excess wording from your text and speed your sentences.

11. Editing Part 2; a system for self-editing and accepting critiques from others

Appendix

Background: The following columns were written when I was chief of a suburban news bureau for *The Indianapolis Star* from 1995 through 2001. Most of my columns pertained to issues in our three-county coverage area, but I sprinkled in family-related columns and a lighter feature. I thought those worked best here.

My first example, headlined *"Wife's Return to Work Tests Dad's Mettle,"* published when our daughter, Kelsey, was 6 years old. It follows:

Column #1 — November 1, 1995

OK, OK, I admit it.

I sent my son to school in his pajamas. Once.

They say that elephants never forget. As tens of thousands of husbands will attest, neither do wives.

Mine throws this story up to me periodically when my ego reaches "need to deflate" mode. It's an episode not easily explained, although gee, those sure looked like sweatpants I was putting on a kindergartner at the time.

I put those PJs on our firstborn, by the way, because our second-born was about to enter the world at St. Vincent Hospital and my betrothed couldn't reach across the county from her hospital bed to do the job. Dad was left behind to attend to chores that, well, he doesn't attend to very often.

That's because, ahem, I have been off at work all these years. Meanwhile, my wonderful bride made the sacrifice to stay home and raise our kids.

(Caution: Do not read this to mean that I went to work and she "just" stayed home. The blunder of saying "You don't work?" to a stay-at-home mom will incur wrath that even a dozen sessions with *"Star Trek"* Counselor Deanna Troi couldn't take the edge off of. Sound red alert and duck out of sight immediately if you are in the room when this happens.)

My fumbling of domestic duties has gotten me out of many a household task over the years. But something traumatic happened to break my streak this fall when our baby daughter started boarding the bus for first grade:

My Wife Went Back to Work! (Outside the Home)

Forget the great pajama caper of '89. A bit of coaching has prepared me to get our little girl ready for school in the hour left once son and Mrs. R have departed for school and, well, school (she's substitute teaching).

Besides, what could there be to the job, with clothes laid out and the lunchbox already filled?

"All you have to do is comb her hair and get her to the bus by 8:30."

A snap.

Never mind that our little one has a blond mane that would make a young Crystal Gayle proud. This is one simple chore: allow a 15-minute cushion, and she'll be the first one at the bus stop.

8:15 a.m. — Brushing is about to begin when we reach our first "snag."

"That's not my favorite brush," she protests.

"What difference does it make?"

A lot of difference, I am advised. So the hunt for favorite brush begins.

8:20 a.m. — Still plenty of time. Favorite brush has been found, let the combing begin.

"I have to go to the bathroom."

8:22 a.m. — Dad: "Sit still, let's get this over with."

The threat to cut her hair if she won't quit griping is utilized (I stole this one from my better half's bag of tricks, having seen it successfully employed on several occasions.")

8:23 a.m. — Uh-oh.

Brush meets sticky blue substance in hair. Is it gum? Candy? Nope.

Just as bad.

Toothpaste.

8:23:01 a.m. — Tug of brush in toothpaste-gooey hair elicits shriek of pain not heard since dino gobbled lawyer in *"Jurassic Park."*

Daughter's head spins around quicker than Linda Blair's in the classic scene from *"The Exorcist."* Scornful glare makes it clear that making up for this one will require letting her stay up past bedtime for a month.

8:29:59 a.m. — Frantic effort to rub toothpaste away, minimize further snags and placate raging 6-year-old gets her pointed to the door. Comber's deodorant has lost the battle in record time this day.

8:45 a.m. — Bus driver arrives. In the meantime, daughter's chasing of other kids at the bus stop has hair flying every which direction. Brushing was pointless.

8:46 a.m. — Dad turns back inside to lock the doors and head for work.

But he pauses.

It's sure quiet in here.

This will take getting used to.

Column #2 — October 30, 1996

Background: Here's a column from when our son was 13 years old. It was headlined:
"Soccer Coaching Stint Was Tough, But What a Kick it Was."

A good friend recently found himself between jobs. The company he worked for couldn't stop its sales from plummeting, so he and many others were thrown out of work.

Fortunately, at least in his case, the joblessness didn't last long. He's bound for Minneapolis and an even better opportunity, plus a nice home for his family.

Before he landed his new position, there was queasiness and uncertainty. But there also was some sunshine that managed to peek through the gloom.

For all bad comes something good, or so it's said. In my friend's case, it was more time to spend with his children.

"For a month, I got to see all of Matt's baseball games," he told me, and there was more talk of finding time down the road to try to coach one of Matt's teams.

My advice? Do it.

Take it from a guy who used to beg off when the idea was suggested.

"Too busy. I can come to the games, but I'll never get all my work done with all the practices, planning, calling the players.

"I can be an assistant coach and help out a little, maybe, but head coach? Sorry."

Sound familiar?

Then maybe you're like me, and my friend. We love our kids, of course. But a sense of duty to work often keeps us from coming home right on time. It finds us toting home a briefcase with just enough tasks inside to stay "caught up." It squeezes out some time for other things that shouldn't be squeezed out.

But I was lucky this year.

My son Andrew signed up to play soccer, but no one jumped at the chance to be head coach. This time I couldn't handle the double-team pressure from my wife, Ginger, and the Fishers Youth Soccer League.

So off I went, Vince Lombardi and John Wooden rolled into one, save one tiny problem: I didn't know a whole lot about soccer. I found myself confronted by 15 boys, ages 10 to 13, who sensed that within 20 seconds of our opening practice.

I did a lot of bluffing that first day. "Tyler, show us the proper way to make a throw-in," I bellowed, then had the nerve to say, "Pretty good," and critique his effort.

Truth be told, he should have been doing the critiquing.

Yet it wasn't long before I was checking out "how-to" soccer books and a wonderful video from the Fishers Library. I leaned on other dads to soak up what they knew and spent hours at home sifting possible lineups and formations. I pestered one of the newspaper's ad reps, Justin Clevenger, who played soccer for Butler University, to the point where Justin must have dreaded my approach.

The real lessons, though, came from the kids. Blue Thunder, they named themselves, after the color of their jerseys.

All were upbeat, enthusiastic, devilishly mischievous at times, fun-loving, and high on life. I looked forward to every one of the 18 times we practiced or played, and even though our last game was played over a week ago, I miss the team already.

I'll remember the gutsy goalkeeper who was knocked down by an opposing player in a frightful collision. The same goalie bounced back to make several saves the next time he manned the net.

I'll remember how our kids playfully stuck the nickname "Chuck" on a lad who lost his breakfast after sprinting all over the field during one 8 a.m. game. And I'll remember consoling players, including my son, who allowed the other team to score.

I'll remember asking my players, as our final game was about to start, who would set the example that day by playing his hardest. Every player's hand shot up, and they did.

I'd like to say we were league champions, but we weren't. We won more than we lost and we tied a few games.

At the team "banquet" (Pizza Hut), the coach told the players and their parents he was grateful for the experience and offered a condensed version of what he's written here.

Moral of the story? It should happen to you.

Don't be "too busy." Grab at the chance, while you still can.

Column #3—November 4, 1997

Background: Former major league pitcher Carl Erskine of Anderson gave me several interviews, and I marveled at his sense of humor and welcoming personality. This is one of my favorites, headlined:

"Ex-pitcher Carl Erskine Recalls Day When Numeral 5 Seemed Magical"

You're vacationing a thousand miles away when you chance upon your next-door neighbors. You're playing cards and the same hand is dealt to you twice in a row.

Most of us have experienced remarkable coincidences. But you'd have to go some to top the story Carl Erskine told me over lunch last week in Anderson.

Erskine has had an "amazing but true" sort of life in the first place. He pitched for one of the better major league baseball teams of the 20th century, the Brooklyn Dodgers of the 1950s. Among his teammates were Jackie Robinson, Gil Hodges, Pee Wee Reese, Duke Snider, and Roy Campanella.

Carl came home to Anderson to finish his education, work his way up to bank president, and contribute to his community in numerous other ways. He and his wife, Betty, celebrated their 50th wedding anniversary less than a month ago, on Oct. 5.

It is that number—5—that is at the heart of this story.

"I made two starts in the 1952 World Series," he recalled. "The second one came in the fifth game at

Yankee Stadium, which happened to be the date of our fifth wedding anniversary.

"When I arrived that day, there was a telegram on the stool in front of my locker. It came from someone in Texas.

"It said, 'Good luck in this fifth game on the 5th of October, and congratulations on your fifth wedding anniversary."

Erskine didn't think much of it at that moment. He had once played at Fort Worth in the Texas League, so well-wishes from there weren't unusual.

The afternoon game started and the Dodgers staked Erskine to the lead. "I had very good stuff and pitched well until the *fifth* inning," he reminisced. "Then the Yankees scored—how many—five runs."

"Oisk," as he was affectionately known to Brooklyn fans, had surrendered a few cheap hits, a walk or two, and a mammoth homer to Johnny Mize. Now the Dodgers trailed, 5-4, and out to the mound came Brooklyn manager Charlie Dressen, presumably to remove his pitcher.

"He asked for the ball—always a bad sign—and says to me, 'Are you all right?' I was downhearted, and said I was."

By this time, the entire Dodger infield had gathered around Dressen and Erskine.

"Then he asked—and this floored me—'Is this your wedding anniversary?' I was shocked. Then he said, 'Is your wife here? Are you going to celebrate tonight?' It was really off the wall. I couldn't believe these questions."

Erskine, resigned to heading for the showers, said Dressen instead surprised him by returning the ball with a final comment: "See if you can get the side out before it gets dark."

Erskine did retire Yogi Berra on a fly ball to end the inning and was surprised again when Dressen didn't remove him for a pinch-hitter.

On and on he pitched. His teammates tied the score in the seventh. Then in the 11th, his roommate, Duke Snider, drove in a run to put Brooklyn ahead.

"I go out to pitch the bottom of the 11th and get the first two guys out. Now Berra is up again with two strikes, but I've got a blister on my finger.

"I threw him the best curve I could, and he took it for strike three to end the game! On that pitch, the blister broke completely off. I couldn't have thrown another pitch."

Nineteen straight Yankees had been retired since Mize's home run. Erskine finished the story with a flourish:

"Because of all the fives that day, I had been watching for anything possible to do with that number 5 by that point.

"I looked at the clock when Berra took the third strike.

"It was five minutes past 5."

Column #4—October 7, 1997

Background: Daughter Kelsey was 8 when I wrote it. This piece was headlined:

"Fries, Carrots, and Beautiful Young Ladies Create Memories."

It took me 40 years to be able to sit at the same lunch table as all the pretty girls.

But don't get the wrong idea. When it happened last week, I was two feet taller than all of them and, well, 40 years older.

The scene: Fishers Elementary School.

The dining partners: daughter Kelsey and her third-grade classmates.

The reason: wife Ginger suggested it for my midweek day off, one of so many floating holidays I've procrastinated about taking but need to squeeze in before the end of the year.

Ginger's was one of those "suggestions" that only Richard the Lion-Hearted would consider answering in the negative.

It fell in the same category as "Sure would be nice if you could help vacuum this weekend," or "Somebody needs to do the trimming."

Not that I mind going to visit Kelsey at lunch, gosh no. It's just that I don't always think of these things, and sleeping in followed by further rest on the sofa seemed such a good idea.

Instead, I found myself towering above the rest of the lunch line, being absorbed by dozens of sets of little eyes with "What's he doing here?" looks.

One of my first surprises, after paying for my $1.95 adult meal and having my hamburger dished up, was being offered a choice by the server: French fries or carrot sticks?

French fries or carrot sticks?

To someone like me, who turned up his nose as every passing vegetable for the first 12 years of life and assumed other kids did the same, the option seemed a little like, "Free ticket to Disney World or poke in the eye with a stick?"

I mean, surely they're cooking hundreds of pounds of fries and slicing what, two or three carrots for the whole school district?

Imagine my surprise to hear that's not necessarily the case. And to see that our elementary school has...a salad bar. And to spot that at least three of Kelsey's eight or nine tablemates this day have the salads on their trays, bypassing the burger and fries offering.

Zounds!

There wasn't any salad bar in the elementary school days of my past. There was the option of going home for lunch. To this day, I can smell the soup and taste my mom's fresh sandwiches.

Alas, those days are all but gone. Most public school districts I'm aware of prohibit kids from even walking to school, let alone walking home to lunch.

One tradition that has carried forth these 40 years is the all-boys, all-girls seating arrangement at most tables.

Another element that jumps out at you in the Fishers Elementary cafeteria is the replica of a stop sign on the far wall.

If it's green, that means the kids are behaving themselves. Flick to yellow, and it's getting noisy.

Should the light turn red, they put the cuffs on.

Just kidding, Principal Munson. I wanted to see if you were still reading.

The food was tasty (those fries, especially), and the conversation of my dining companions wide-ranging and quite frank, though a bit giggly at times.

Best part of the experience? Kelsey's happy smile greeting me when she saw me arrive.

Thanks to Mrs. Royalty for her gentle nudge, getting me to the school lunch line while there's still time to enjoy the experience.

Things should be different in just a few years. At junior high age, Kelsey will no doubt be mortified if I try a lunchtime visit in front of her friends.

For now, it's a special memory. If you're a parent of an elementary school child, take the day off, dig out your buck-ninety-five and go make a memory of your own.

***

Afterword

The decline of the newspaper industry has been one of the sadder developments in my life.

I thought I would eventually retire from newspapers when I took my first job writing sports for the Bloomington *Courier-Tribune* in 1971. Changes fueled by the explosion of Internet sites, TV coverage, and the 24-hour news cycle altered my destiny.

I left newspapering after 30 years for an exciting opportunity in communications with Eli Lilly and Company. I made my escape before the livelihoods of so many newspaper friends were subjected to layoffs, buyouts, or mandatory time off without pay.

Journalists' jobs were slashed as newspapers shuttered or became a shriveled version of their former selves. Circulation plummeted while reading habits changed. Consolidation turned many if not most newspapers that survived into profit-driven enterprises, pleasing shareholders above the needs of their own staffs.

This book includes anecdotes from my newspaper career. You might see similar anecdotes about the news business today, but they're told electronically, on tight budgets, and by newspapers surviving with a fraction of their previous staffs.

Electronic newsgathering comes from a multitude of talented journalists. News websites kept many papers afloat as they joined the electronic party, catering to online preferences.

The best of all these journalists convey truth without an agenda. They don't root for a particular party or candidate. They allow opinions only when they are clearly labeled as such.

This doesn't mean to ignore commentary, but to judge it against facts gathered in an unbiased way.

Society needs talented, committed journalists more than ever. Freedom of the press is what distinguishes the United States from the likes of China and Russia. Their regimes believe in "killing the messenger," replacing a free press with dictated propaganda.

We are *so* fortunate as a country. The best of the independent media are indispensable, keeping tabs on how our tax dollars are spent, uncovering excesses, and exposing those who capitalize on the underprivileged or the unaware. Infallible? No, just like other institutions. But our free press keeps us informed and, on the best days, serves as a conscience for our free country, especially in hard times like the COVID pandemic.

I hope with all my heart that responsible delivery of news will never go out of business.

***

This book took much longer to prepare than I would have imagined. The old saw, "nothing good comes easy" applies.

Of course you, the reader, determine how interesting and worthwhile these writings have been.

If you enjoy the work, then give my wife, Ginger, a heap of credit. As I have noted, she's been my "first read" for decades. Many, many thanks, Mrs. R. Not only did you contribute mightily here, but of course you gave life to Andrew and Kelsey—our greatest legacy. We are so proud of them.

Friends Vic and Linda Caleca provided valuable edits and, in Vic's case, a book title. Dan Carpenter, another pal and *Indianapolis Star* alum, offered encouragement from his perspective as a published author.

Talented St. Louis journalist Ron Cobb was among my first editors on the Bob Knight chapter. We were staff mates and friends at the *Courier-Tribune* long ago, though our friendship remains fresh.

Marilyn Irwin also had good advice for the Knight chapter. She and husband Paul and another close buddy, John Messina, provided inspiration.

In the first chapter, I quoted Jack Backer's oft-spoken phrase, "Progress is Crisis-Oriented," which is so true. Jack died way too young after teaching and encouraging me among thousands of other Indiana University journalism students. Ralph Holsinger and Will Counts of IU also were important influences in my life, as was the remarkable Marge Blewett.

At *The Indianapolis Star*, my positive influences were many. I've mentioned Larry Connor, Helen Connor, Tom Keating, and there were many more.

We moved to Prescott Valley, Arizona, in 2016 following my retirement from Eli Lilly and Company, where I learned much from good friends Rob Friedman,

David Marbaugh, and others. Here in AZ, the Central Arizona Writers group has helped keep my writing fires aflame. Special thanks to the group's president, Pat Fogarty.

I can't name all the other positive influences without leaving out someone, so I won't try other than to say that great teachers, reporters, editors, writing coaches and acquaintances have enriched my life. I can't fully repay them all, but I hope this book is a start.

***

I also need to thank Purdue University for the use of photos in the Janice Voss chapter, specifically Andy Hancock for the picture of Janice speaking on campus and Mark Simons for the picture of the VOSS solar system exhibit. NASA provided the photo of Janice in uniform.

About the Author

Dennis Royalty (Dennis Michael Royalty) was born September 23, 1949, in Marion, Indiana. For years some people referred to him as "Junior," unaware that his father, also Dennis M. Royalty, was not Dennis Sr., but rather Dennis Marion Royalty.

Older Dennis was a personnel manager, which was the precursor to what is now known as a manager of human resources. His job moves took his wife, Kathleen, and sons Dennis and David Royalty to several places with him. The family lived on Long Island, New York; Niles, Ohio; and at Littleton, Colorado, before returning to Indiana (Frankfort) in 1964.

It was in Frankfort where the author of this book realized he was on a path to study journalism at Indiana University, his dad's alma mater. Young Dennis was editor of the Frankfort High School newspaper, The High Life, and earned scholarships to IU summer journalism workshops.

Graduating from IU in 1971 after reporting and editing for The Indiana Daily Student newspaper, Dennis Michael Royalty spent three years as a sportswriter for the former *Bloomington Courier-Tribune* and then 27 more (1974-2001) at *The Indianapolis Star*. Over that time he was a bureau reporter, state editor, city editor, features editor, and a bureau chief/columnist.

Dennis thought that newspaper work would be his life's work. But he reluctantly sought a new job (see the Afterword in this book for the reasons why) and was hired by Indianapolis-based pharmaceutical giant Eli Lilly and Company in 2001. Royalty worked in internal communications for Lilly until retiring in 2015.

Royalty and his wife, Ginger, have a son, Andrew, and a daughter, Kelsey. Having dreamed of living in the West in retirement, Dennis and Ginger moved to Prescott Valley, Arizona, in 2016.

Made in the USA
Middletown, DE
26 May 2021